A New Most Excellent Dancing Master

The Journal of Joseph Lowe's visits to
Balmoral and Windsor (1852 - 1860)
to teach dance to the family of
Queen Victoria

Frontispiece. Royal Family Group, 1854
From left, the Prince of Wales, the Princess Royal, Princess Alice, Queen Victoria, and Prince Alfred.

Photographer: Roger Fenton. Copyright Windsor Castle. Royal Archives. (c) 1991. Her Majesty The Queen.

A New Most Excellent Dancing Master

The Journal of Joseph Lowe's visits to Balmoral and Windsor (1852–1860) to teach dance to the family of Queen Victoria

edited by

ALLAN THOMAS

DANCE & MUSIC SERIES No. 5

PENDRAGON PRESS
STUYVESANT, NEW YORK

Other Titles in the DANCE & MUSIC Series

No. 1 *French Court Dance and Dance Music: A Guide to Primary Source Writings 1643-1789* by Judith L. Schwartz and Christena L. Schlundt (1987) ISBN 0-918728-72-X

No. 2. *Dance and Instrumental* Diferencias *in Spain During the 17th and Early 18th Centuries* by Maurice Esses, Vol. I: *History and Background, Music and Dance*, (1992) ISBN 0-945193-08-4

No. 3 *Rhythm and Life: The Work of Emile Jaques-Dalcroze* by Irwin Spector (1990) ISBN 0-945193-00-9

No. 4. *Fifteenth-Century Dance and Music* Vol. I, *The Compete Transcribed Treatises and Collections in the Domenico Piacenza Tradition* translated and annotated by A. William Smith, (1992) ISBN 0-945193-25-4

No. 6. *A Work Book by Kellom Tomlinson: Commonplace Book of an 18th-Century English Dancing Master, A Facsimile Edition* edited by Jennifer Shennan (1992), ISBN 0-945193-31-9

Library of Congress Cataloging-in-Publication Data

Lowe, Joseph, 1797-1866.
    A new most excellent dancing master : the journal of Joseph Lowe's visits tyo Balmoral and Windsor (1852-1860) to teach dance to the family of Queen Victoria / edited by Allan Thomas.
       p. cm. -- (Dance and music series ; no. 5)
    ISBN 0-945193-30-0
    1. Lowe, Joseph, 1797-1866--Diaries. 2. Dance teachers-Scotland-Diaries. 3. Victoria, Queen of Great Britain, 1819-1901--Family. I. Thomas, Allan, 1942- . II. Title. III. Series.
GV1785.L69A3 1992
792.8'028'092--dc20
[B]   92-13521
                                                                  CIP

Copyright 1992 Pendragon Press

TABLE OF CONTENTS

Illustrations	vii
Acknowledgements	ix
Dedication	x
INTRODUCTION	
Introduction	1
The Fiddle	3
The Lowe Family	4
Exercises and Dancing	5
Scottish Dance	9
Queen Victoria's Court and the decade to 1860	10
The Journal	14
The modern edition	14
THE JOURNAL	
I. Mr Lowe's First Visit to Balmoral to teach the Royal Children to Dance, September 16th, 1852	21
II. Mr Lowe's First Visit to Windsor Castle to teach the Royal Family in 1852	32
III. Second Visit to Balmoral to teach the Royal Children in 1853	40
IV. Second Visit to Windsor Castle to teach the Royal Children Dancing and Calisthenic Exercises in 1853	50
V. Third Visit to Balmoral to teach the Royal Children Dancing and Calisthenics in September 1854	59
VI. Third Visit to Windsor Castle to teach the Royal Children in 1854 and 1855	63

TABLE OF CONTENTS

VII. Mr Lowe's Fourth Visit to Balmoral to teach Dancing and Calisthenic Exercises in September 1855	70
VIII. Mr and Miss Lowe's Fourth Visit to Windsor to teach the Royal Family Dancing and Exercises in 1855 and 1856	79
IX. Fifth Visit to Balmoral to teach the Royal Children 1856	89
X. Fifth Visit to teach the Royal Children at Windsor Castle in 1856	89
XI. Sixth Visit to Balmoral to teach the Royal Children in 1857	93
XII. Visit to Windsor in 1857 and 1858 to teach the Royal Children	101
XIII. Balmoral in 1858	107
XIV. Visit to Windsor Castle in 1859 and 1860 to teach the Royal Children	109
XV. Balmoral in 1860	112
XVI. Visit to Windsor Castle in 1860 and 1861	113
APPENDICES	
1. Obituary: "The Late Mr Joseph Lowe"	117
2. "The Balmoral Castle Quadrille" by Joseph Lowe.	118
3a. Family Tree: The Royal Family mentioned in Lowe Journal.	126
3b. Three generations of the Lowe family.	128
4. Members of the Royal Household mentioned in the Lowe Journal.	130
5. Music and Dance Index	132
Bibliography	134

LIST OF ILLUSTRATIONS

Frontispiece, Royal Family Group, 1854.	ii
1. Title page of *Lowes' Ball-Conductor and Assembly Guide* (actual size).	6
2. Illustration from Thomas Wilson's *Companion to the Ball Room* (1817).	8
3. The Journal of Joseph Lowe, two facsimile pages: "Third Visit to Windsor Castle...1854 and 1855."	16, 17
4. The old Castle at Balmoral, September 1854.	20
5. "The Five True Positions" from *Lowes' Ball-Conductor and Assembly Guide*.	23
6. "The Reel of Tulloch," from *The Royal Collection of Reels, Strathspeys and Jigs* by Joseph Lowe.	28
7. Joseph Lowe's advertisement in *The Scotsman*, Saturday 25th September, 1852.	31
8a. "The Princess Alice's Jig" by Joseph Lowe from *The Royal Collection...*	37
8b. The Princess Royal and Princess Alice, 1855 (inset).	37
9a. "Prince Alfred's Reel" by Joseph Lowe from *The Royal Collection...*	42
9b. Prince Alfred, 1854 (inset).	42
10. The new Balmoral Castle from the opposite side of the River Dee, 1857.	45
11a. "The Prince of Wales Jig" by Joseph Lowe from *The Royal Collection...*	48
11a. The Prince of Wales and Prince Alfred, 1855 (inset).	48
12. Queen Victoria, 1855.	52

LIST OF ILLUSTRATIONS

13. Princess Louise and Princess Helena, 1859.	54
14. Queen Victoria in a carriage accompanied by the Princess Royal, the Prince of Wales and Princess Alice, February 10th 1857.	58
15. Queen Victoria's Christmas Tree and table of presents, 1857.	66
16. Joseph Lowe's Receipt for the payment for two visits in 1854.	69
17. The Prince of Wales, Prince Albert and others,1857.	72
18. Royal Family Group, 1855.	76
19. The Princess Royal and Prince Frederick William of Prussia, 1859.	78
20."The Balmoral Castle Quadrille."	80
21. Musician: William Ross, the Queen's Piper, 1855.	82
22. The Journal of Joseph Lowe, facsimile from 3rd January 1856.	86
23a. "Prince Arthur's First Jig in 1858" by Joseph Lowe from *The Royal Collection*...	95
23b. Prince Arthur, 1857 (inset).	95
24. "Sir Roger de Coverley" from Joseph Lowe's *The Royal Collection*. . .	98
25. Title page of *The Royal Collection of Reels, Strathspeys and Jigs, 1859*.	102
26. The Journal of Joseph Lowe, facsimile page: "Balmoral in 1858."	106
27. Interior of a tent erected at Balmoral for a Ball, 1868.	108
28. Royal Family Group, Buckingham Palace, 1860.	112

ACKNOWLEDGMENTS

I am grateful to the Lowe and Trimmer families for their confidence and interest in this publication, and in particular to Pamela Cooper (née Lowe), the owner of the manuscript.

Dr. Alastair MacFadyen, formerly Honorary Archivist of the Royal Scottish Country Dance Society, generously made his own researches on the Lowe family available and provided a perspective for the work from Edinburgh.

Jennifer Shennan worked with me on the initial deciphering of the Journal, word by word, and has written the dance descriptions. A British Council grant assisted her researches in Britain, 1990-91.

The Royal Archives, Windsor Castle (Deputy Registrar Miss Pamela Clark and Miss Frances Dimond) have been most helpful in locating the materials from Queen Victoria's unpublished Journals, identifying members of the Royal Household, and in selecting suitable photographs from the extensive collections. The extracts from Queen Victoria's Journals are included in this edition by gracious permission of Her Majesty Queen Elizabeth II.

Librarians worldwide have answered calls for help in locating the Lowes published material: I would like to acknowledge those in Wellington (Victoria University), Washington DC (the Library of Congress), New York (Dance Collection of the New York Public Library at the Lincoln Centre), London (the Music Room of the British Library) and Edinburgh (the National Library of Scotland). In particular Margaret Calder, Chief Librarian of the Turnbull Library, National Library of New Zealand, and the staff of the library who now care for the manuscript, provided assistance and support.

Illustrations and quotations from *Lowes' Ball-Conductor and Assembly Guide* and *The Balmoral Castle Quadrille* are included by kind permission of the Trustees of the National Library of Scotland; and the music from *The Royal Collection of Reels, Strathspeys and Jigs*, by Joseph Lowe, by permission of the British Library.

ACKNOWLEDGMENTS

Individuals, mostly in Wellington, whom I wish to thank for their inspiration, and their technical skills include: Dr John Mansfield Thomson, Edith Lauder Campbell, Mrs Sheila McKenzie (Register House, Edinburgh), Dr Laurie Bauer, John Casey and Brett Robertson (photographers), and Michele Power (word processing).

Background articles on the Lowe family history and the dance manuscripts and books of the Lowe collection will be assembled in loate 1992 in conjunction with an exhibition at the National Library of New Zealand, P.O. Box 12-349, Wellington, New Zealand.

I thank Wendy Hilton and Robert Kessler of Pendragon Press for their encouragement and skill, and my wife Jennifer, and daughters Nell and Beth, for all their assitance and patience. To all readers, I hope you enjoy, as I have, time in the company of Mr Joseph Lowe.

Allan Thomas
Victoria University of Wellington
February 1992

This Book is Dedicated to the Memory of

PAMELA DOROTHY LOWE, née TRIMMER (1925–1978)

It was due to Pamela's commitment and involvement with dance that the Lowe family book collection was maintained. It was her long cherished hope to see the various manuscripts researched and published and her family remembers her with love on this occasion.

INTRODUCTION

Queen Victoria's Journal records that on the 20th September 1852 at Balmoral Castle, she "took a few minutes lesson in reel dancing with Mr Lowe, a new, most excellent master." Eight years later, on 3rd January 1860 at Windsor Castle, she "Joined, as I have many days, in the reel dancing at the children's lessons with Mr Lowe." These Journal entries frame the period of Joseph Lowe's 16 teaching visits in which the Royal Children and their parents, together with some relations, staff and friends, learn the basic steps and figures of the Reels and Quadrilles. There is romping for the younger children to Pop Goes the Weasel; there are exercises for fitness and deportment and, for the older children, some more specialised dances and a chance to show their accomplishments at the Court Balls and Tenantry dances. The Queen danced for only a few minutes in 1852 but in 1860

> they all danced together for an hour. The Queen, the Princess Alice, Prince of Wales and my daughter danced the Reel of Tulloch with great spirit, swinging each other without ceremony sometimes rather too roughly and with too much force for such a slippery floor, but they all seemed to enjoy it very much. (Lowe Journal 3 January 1860).

The Journal of these years by Joseph Lowe is an engaging portrait of this hard working dancing master in the mid 19th century, with his fiddle for accompaniment, his repertoire of dances, his recreations in fishing, walking, fiddling, and the occasional toddy before bed. He teaches the dances and the physical exercises with care and commitment, he fishes with the Royal Princes with unsurpassed skill, he endures a freezing train journey without undue complaint, and he values the personal contacts he has with his pupils in the Royal Family, with the other staff at Balmoral and Windsor, and with his own family and friends. His is an intimate picture of Court life, a "view from below." He records, for example, that in the Reel of Thulichan, the 12 year old "Princess Royal got a dreadful fall and skinned her elbow, she did not cry but her eyes filled with tears" (24 September 1853). But he does not record, and may not have known, that the Prince of Prussia, who visits in September 1855 with a considerable retinue, became engaged to be married to the Princess

INTRODUCTION

Royal in a match that it was feared would not be popular in England or Germany; the engagement was in fact concealed from the public for twenty months. Famous men of the day appear at Court, the Prime Minister Lord Aberdeen, the veteran soldier General Hardinge, but if their business was known (perhaps to tender a resignation or to advise on the progress of the Crimean War), Lowe does not record it.

We do learn though, in an account which is a treasure of musical literature, of Lowe's feelings as a professional musician assisting in a very poor band engaged for the Ball in September 1857. We see through Lowe's eyes, in the Kitchen, the Great Hall and the Dining Room, the awe-inspiring sight of the gold plate, tapestries and other treasures of the Castle, and the Christmas Tree that was to become established as a popular custom throughout the English speaking world. Lowe enjoys the celebrity concerts and theatricals which were features of the New Year festivities at Court at this time. And he is a participant in the comprehensive educational programme set up by Queen Victoria and Prince Albert for the needs of their large family. Although Lowe has the full confidence of the Queen during this important decade, others of Scotland's finest dance and music exponents are also employed at various times in Victoria's enthusiasm for the Scottish dance—Andrew Thomson teaches at Balmoral in 1849–1851, James Scott Skinner teaches the Tenantry on the Queen's Estate, Alexander Walker and Willie Blair play in the bands.

Lowe's Journal also provides a portrait of the Royal Family at this time; always deferential, sometimes perceptive. The manner and concerns of Prince Albert and the Queen and the emerging personalities of the children, each destined for a public career, may be glimpsed. Albert, known for his efficiencies in the running of the Royal establishments and for his involvement with the children's education (from playing with blocks to deciding when they should begin Latin) is revealed here as a master of the one-liner. Lowe is often greeted by a cheerful quip from the Prince: when out walking in deep snow at the Farm (6th January 1854) Prince Albert says, "I hope you are not in your dancing pumps Mr Lowe," and in showing the new Ball Room at Balmoral Albert teases, "This is to be your apartment Mr Lowe" (22 September 1854).

Joseph Lowe, considered to be the leading Scottish dancing master of his day, led a busy professional life. The visits to Balmoral and Windsor recorded in this Journal occurred as intervals in his regular teaching periods in Inverness in the summer months, and in Edinburgh for the remainder of the year. When the Queen requests that Lowe come to Windsor in mid-January, rather than in the Christmas-New Year holiday, he gives the straightforward answer that he cannot manage this as January is his "busiest time" (22 September 1852). Lowe is a composer and arranger of dance tunes, with an extensive published collection. He directs his own Dance Academy and he plays in the band for balls. A dancing master, he is equally proficient in music and dance, and central to all his activities is the violin or "fiddle."

The Fiddle

For Joseph Lowe the fiddle was both the instrument of dance accompaniment in Lessons and Balls, and also a principal recreation and pleasure. Many days are rounded out with playing: "had tea, then commenced fiddling and spent a happy evening" (29 December 1855). Partners in this music making are Mr Menzies, whom Lowe describes as "a genuine Scotsman fond of fiddling" (5 January 1852), and Willie Blair, who was popularly known as the Queen's Fiddler. Blair was evidently an exuberant companion who on a fishing expedition "got into a farm house with some of the Gillies and got himself quite spoiled . . . I had to hire a Gig to take him home" (23 September 1853) (see also illustration 18, caption). On one occasion Lowe relates that he and Mr Menzies travelling from Windsor to London "got a second class carriage to ourselves. I opened my fiddle box and fiddled all the way" (7 January 1857).

But Lowe also frequently plays alone for his own enjoyment: "read, wrote and fiddled the whole evening and to bed by ten" (26 September 1857). When the solo fiddle is played thus, away from the dance, one may assume that there is embellishment of the dance tune. Some of the riches of the variation form developed in Scotland as recital music in the previous century may well have survived in this playing. Whether in the solitary or in social playing, or in accompaniment of dance, the playing by Lowe and the other fiddlers would have been zestful and lively. The short bows, accents, shakes, glides and other ornaments gave this music an energy which fully accompanied the vigorous dance.

Lowe's extensive involvement with music publication does not catch the brilliance of such improvisatory performance, but presents simple settings of the dance tunes, for pianoforte playing.[1] Lowe provides rudimentary accompaniment for the tune in his publications which is often reminiscent of

---

[1] A number of Lowe's compositions are included as illustrations (see Music and Dance Index) and the complete Balmoral Quadrille in the Appendix.

INTRODUCTION

the drone played by bagpipes or suggested on the violin open strings. On several visits to Windsor a pianoforte is hired for use at the lodgings, but there is no reference to its use in dance accompaniment. Some of the dance tunes are dedicated by permission to members of the Royal family, a common form of patronage for many teachers including Andrew Thomson Lowe's predecessor as dance teacher at Balmoral.

The violin remains the supreme instrument for dance accompaniment, capable of strongly rhythmical as well as intensely lyrical playing. With it the dancing master had a commanding presence, able to see his dancers and simultaneously shape the music to their needs. In Lowe's account of a Ball at Balmoral in September 1857 these qualities are reaffirmed:

> My fiddle spoke out beautifully [in the dance] and I kept it up with spirit till the end. The leader expressed himself surprised at my lasting qualities and of the power of my fiddle. (29 September 1857)

In this remark Joseph may also have been extolling the fine Scottish School of violin making, though unfortunately we do not know the provenance of his instruments.

Lowe's musical activities also include composition of his own dance tunes, teaching the fiddle to Prince Arthur and son Johnnie, and writing out dance tunes for the pipers. He is thoroughly the classical dancing master, versed both in music and dance, following the tradition of the dancing masters of the preceding century.

The Lowe Family[2]

Joseph is accompanied on all but four of his 16 teaching visits by one of his children, Charlotte or Johnnie or Euphemia, who assist him at the lessons by demonstrating the dances and exercises or by partnering the Royal Children. The presence of Lowe's children formed a particularly warm bond with the Royal Family, expressed in the presents given and good wishes frequently offered. In 1856 Lowe is unable to go to Balmoral but "Miss Lowe and my son Robert went and were very kindly received." After Joseph's last visit in 1860 the Royal Archives records that the Misses Lowe continued teaching from 1863 until 1873, but no account of their activities has been found.

---

[2]Three generations of the Lowe Family Tree are shown in Appendix 3b.

The Journal occasionally provides glimpses of Lowe's adult family—his daughter Mary returning from Brussels, his son John released from a shipping indenture. But it is not always clear who are family members and who are friends; indeed Mrs Robson, the great friend mentioned on each visit to London, becomes Charlotte's mother-in-law in 1867. Her son, Mr. Frederick Robson, who visits the Lowes at Windsor in 1857 is described on the marriage certificate as "Surgeon, late of Shanghai."

There are prominent dancing masters in the Lowe family who are not part of the Journal record—Joseph's three brothers, and Joseph's son, Joseph Eager Lowe. During the Journal years, Joseph Eager Lowe married and emigrated to New Zealand, and thence to Australia, where he set up a dancing school in Melbourne. It is through the descendants of this Joseph Eager Lowe that the Journal and collection of other dance books and manuscripts has been preserved in New Zealand.

The three members of Joseph's own generation, Robert, J. S. (James), and John Lowe were, with him, co-authors of *Lowes' Ball-Conductor and Assembly Guide* which appeared about 1820 and was reprinted several times. The *Ball-Conductor* (Illustration 1.) gives general principles of etiquette for the Ball or Assembly and is an aide memoire for the dance steps.

Exercises and Dancing

Lowe's approach to dance teaching was well based in an awareness of the importance of general fitness and good deportment, and his teaching seasons were often entered in the Journal as a "Visit to teach Dancing and Calisthenics..." Queen Victoria, an enthusiast for dance, was especially noted for her regal deportment. Although not exactly tall, she nevertheless had a commanding presence, and hoped to instil this quality in her children. She commended the Princess Alice's Spanish Dance as "an excellent exercise for improving the figure and teaching graceful motion" (5 January 1856).

At the Exercise Lessons, Lowe used various types of equipment—chest expanders, clubs, sceptres and the skipping-rope—some of which are credited as his own innovations in dance training. On one occasion Queen Victoria expressed appreciation of certain arm and hand exercises which, although they made her tired, helped to counter the problems she was experiencing with rheumatism in her arms (30 December 1857). One child, Princess Helena, had the persistent fault of "turning in" her left foot. Lowe recorded that both Queen Victoria and Prince Albert commented on this and en-

LOWES'
BALL-CONDUCTOR
AND
ASSEMBLY GUIDE;

CONTAINING

Directions for the Performance

OF

QUADRILLES, GALLOPADES, MAZOURKAS, MESCOLANZES, ECOSSOISES, SPANISH, ENGLISH, IRISH, & SCOTCH COUNTRY DANCES, REELS, &c. &c.

WITH A FEW HINTS

ON

DEPORTMENT AND BALL-ROOM ETIQUETTE,

FOR THEIR JUVENILE PUPILS.

BY THE MESSRS. LOWE,

Teachers of Dancing,

Edinburgh, Glasgow, Perth, Dundee, &c.

THIRD EDITION,
Enlarged and Improved.

—oooo—

EDINBURGH:
PRINTED FOR THE MESSRS. LOWE;
AND SOLD BY THE
MUSIC-SELLERS AND STATIONERS.

---

1. Title page *Lowes' Ball-Conductor and Assembly Guide*

The Ball Conductor was a handy-sized reference work for the steps and formations of dances as well as an extended treatise on the beneficial effects of dancing of more than 170 pages. Hints on Deportment and Ball Room Etiquette abound as "Good manners and good Dancing must go hand in hand" (vi). The Lowes stress "the propriety of sending children to the Dancing School before their joints get stiff, or fixed in an awkward position, and previous to their being engaged with other branches of education that require more attention"(iv), but of avoiding foreign teachers who are supposed "to be clever, because they speak a language . . . which the children do not understand"(v). This is clearly a reference to the dominance of the French influence in dance and dance teaching throughout Europe in the preceeding generations.

couraged the child to correct it (29 September 1854). On another occasion the Queen mimicked the jiggling shoulders of her daughter dancing, likening the effect to that of the "country girls" (3 January 1855). The Royal Physician, Sir James Clark, observed an Exercise Lesson on 29 December 1852 and, although there was no comment from him at the time, he appeared to be impressed. Lowe himself liked to be active and on days when he was not teaching at the Castle he regularly took long walks in the neighbouring countryside and when at Balmoral he frequently went fishing nearby.

Lowe's stamina was impressive. In the first season in 1852 at Balmoral Castle, and at nearby Abergeldie (where the family of the Queen's half sister were staying with the Queen's mother,[3]) Lowe taught on 18 days a total of approximately 80 lessons. Most often individual lessons were given, though at times pairs of names are listed in a way that could mean that some lessons were shared. As well, Lowe accompanied eight general dancing sessions that season in which Queen Victoria and Prince Albert joined. Besides a Ball there were several parties which Lowe attended and, in addition to maintaining this schedule, Lowe on numerous occasions taught exercises to the sons of his friend McDonald. Many of the Household Staff also engaged him for a lesson, sometimes taking even two lessons in one day if the timetable permitted. At these he might be asked to run through some Scotch Steps or the Figures of a dance which would be needed at the Ball that night.

The Journal indicates that Lowe's repertoire included dances of several different kinds: the Country Dances and Reels of Scotland (his pupils' favourites), the fashionable European dances such as Waltzes, Quadrilles and Polkas, and the solo dances such as Highland Fling, Hornpipe, Sword Dance and other character compositions. There were distinct styles of dancing, each with their own conventions and musical accompaniment.

Although only the titles of the dances appear in the Journal, the *Lowes' Ball-Conductor and Assembly Guide* includes them all, and many more besides, with instructions and description of the style and the movement quality proper to each dance type.[4]

The 18th century vogue for French dancing had been widespread and had resulted in various refinements to Scottish dancing in the form of stylized

---

[3] The Royal Family Tree, including Royal relations who are mentioned in the Journal, is given in the Appendix.

[4] The Music and Dance Index gives references to the dances mentioned in the Journal, and the quotations from *Lowes' Ball-Conductor and Assembly Guide*.

2. Illustration from Thomas Wilson's *Companion to the Ball Room* (1817)

The different formations, styles and moods of several dance styles, which Joseph Lowe taught later in the century, are graphically portrayed: in front a lively Reel danced by two couples to the bagpipes, contrasts with an elegant single couple apparently posed in a Minuet; behind is a figured Country dance for four couples in contrast to six couples in a graceful Waltz. Children also take their place on the dance floor, and the different accompaniments for the dances are depicted around the sides of the room—presumably they are not playing or dancing simultaneously!

foot positions, turn-out of the foot, and the leg movements of Highland exhibition dancing. As well, attention to deportment and poise in the social dances of polite company continued to mould dance style. But the love of vigorous movement traditional to the Scots was by no means extinguished in this process. By the late 18th century, in fact, Scottish dances were themselves proving highly fashionable and popular in European courts and the city of Edinburgh became a mecca for visiting professional dance teachers seeking to expand their repertoire with new dances.

Amongst the social group dances of European origin, Quadrilles were square dances for four couples in which set figures were combined in a variety of sequences. They were appreciated for the taste and decorum of their style in contrast to the more spirited Polkas and Galops, Reels and Country Dances.

The Waltz, with its intimate character and graceful turning, does not figure as prominently in the Journal as do Reels and Country Dances, although *Lowes' Ball-Conductor* describes the waltz in some detail, including jump, hop and spring steps. Queen Victoria regretted as a young woman that she could not fully participate in this fashionable new dance as it was considered undignified for the Sovereign to dance in the arms of a subject.

Scottish Dance

Traditional dancing in Scotland involved a plethora of rhythms beaten out by the feet: shuffles, beats extended into kicks, rockings, sheddings, shakes and balances. Included in the Country Dance repertoire were heel stamps, shuffling, trebling or treepling, flegs (fluttering with a swinging step) and fleups (side steps without lifting the feet).

The Highland Reels, with their binding serpentine figures and distinctive setting steps, were certainly the favourite dances during Lowe's years with the Royal Household. The Reel could be danced by couples or by groups, and included virtuoso steps which in the Ball Room would likely be modified, particularly by the Ladies. Queen Victoria did indeed ask Mr Lowe for help with her Scotch Steps on several occasions, and she worried that they were executed with too masculine a style. Lowe repeatedly assures the Queen she is dancing well, then he qualifies this to mean that she is dancing as well as can be expected in view of the very few opportunities she has to practise, and does agree that the steps could be adjusted to suit her! The Queen confides in Lowe that she feels very well so long as she is dancing to the accompaniment of his violin, whereas dancing to the piper, or practising on her own, she is likely to forget the steps altogether.

The Lowe brothers in their *Ball-Conductor* are very particular about the technique of foot movements (see illustration 5 and caption) and also express their distaste for "rude and uncultivated" dance behaviour:

> It would be well if some Gentlemen would give a little more attention to their partner's mode of stepping, and not drag them along as if by force, whilst they themselves are capering, rattling or shuffling their feet in the rudest manner. Such barbarism must be disgusting to every person accustomed to more cultivated conduct, and cannot please any but such who are equally rude with those who are guilty of it. (page 162,163)

In the "Advertisement" in the *Royal Collection of Reels, Strathspeys and Jigs* (1859), Joseph Lowe emphasizes that "it has been his aim for many years to smooth down and assimilate as much as possible the dancing of our Reels and Strathspeys to the style of the present day." His brother Robert expressed a preference for pupils who had been "trained by himself or his Brother or his Nephews, as they have all the same style of stepping." But despite the general refining of the steps into the style deemed appropriate for the polite Ballroom, the Lowe brothers were not content with lifeless dances, they demanded spirited participation from their pupils.

Joseph Lowe's lessons for Queen Victoria suggest a balance being sought between the native dance tradition and the newer social demands of the Ballroom. Dance history everywhere is full of such adjustments, and indeed the vitality of Scottish dance traditions had survived remarkably well the importation of the formal grace of the French minuet in the preceeding generation.

Joseph Lowe was a confident and accomplished dance master, who took great pride in his work and in the success of his pupils. He was a confident keeper of the old traditions and at the same time proficient master of the new.

Queen Victoria's Court and the decade to 1860.

Queen Victoria's Court was alive with music and dance and with enthusiastic participation in new inventions like photography, and was borne along by the momentous events of the day.

Dancing was a principal recreation and delight in Queen Victoria's Court, whether a state occasion at Windsor, a Gillies' Dance at Balmoral, or a lesson for the Royal Children in which the family joined. At a Ball at Balmoral in 1857 the Queen could hardly keep her seat for laughing at Lord Granville's attempts to dance the Highland Fling, and the vigorous attempts of little Prince Arthur to dance the Steps he saw the Highlanders about him doing (23 September 1857). The Gillies had an ongoing tradition of dance, but the Maids of Honour clamoured for dance lessons from Lowe so that they could play their part in Court. The Queen's enthusiasm for dance, well documented in Lowe's Journal, reshaped the Court arts, and was widely influencial in Britain and the Empire.

Lowe has several polite phrases to pass over the monotony of some of the work: "Had the usual lessons; nothing unusual occurred," "Attended at the usual hour, gave all the usual lessons." There is, though, much genuine pleasure and pride in the fact that the Royal Children receive compliments for their dancing in front of guests at the Balls. Both parents repeat to Lowe how pleased they are at this. All the Royal Children are apparently confident and adventurous dancers, as no doubt their parents intended they should be, but Princess Alice clearly has talent and makes rapid progress. She learns the "Spanish Guaracha" complete with castanets and a special Spanish dress for the occasion. (This dance, the Guaracha, a favourite of the time, is listed twice in the Plan for John Lowe's Ball in Perth in 1826 as both a solo and a duet; it also features in the demonstration Ball of the pupils of Mr and the Misses Lowe at the Merchant Maidens' Hospital, Edinburgh, in February 1859.)

In music too the Royal Couple, Victoria and Albert, were keen amateurs, playing and singing privately for their own pleasure, and openly for the Court. Albert was a composer, as was the Queen's mother the Duchess of Kent. Two of the children, Alfred and Beatrice, published music in their adult life. Frequent visitors to the Court were musical celebrities giving recitals often of the latest music. Mendelssohn was a musical confidant of the Queen, and the concert Joseph Lowe attends in 1853, one of the New Year's Concerts by the Queen's Orchestra and Choir, is a first performance of two of Mendelssohn's unfinished works. Mendelssohn was but one of a string of virtuosi who entertained the Royal Family over the years: Edvard Grieg, Paderewski, Jenny Lind "the Swedish Nightingale," Franz Liszt, Sir Arthur Sullivan, Signors Lablache, Leoncavallo, Merio and more. It was a Court which valued both the amateur and professional, domestic music making and that of the virtuoso. "Pop Goes the Weasel," a favourite tune frequently encountered in Lowe's Journal, gained its mid-century popularity (it had a long history as an English folk dance) from the Queen's use of it at Court Balls, as well as from American satirical verses.

INTRODUCTION

The new invention of photography was quickly taken up by Victoria and Albert for recording the family, residences, and events.[5] As well as commissioning and purchasing works of the finest pioneer photographers, Victoria and Albert were informed patrons of the newly formed Photographers' Society, and allowed a portrait of the Queen to be published for the first time in 1860.

The years in which Lowe attends Balmoral and Windsor were perhaps the personal and political zenith of Victoria's Court. In 1851 the Great Exhibition of the Works of Industry of All Nations at the Crystal Palace, which Prince Albert had designed and inspired, was opened. Though the project had been reviled in Parliament and the Press it was a triumphant success which greatly enhanced Albert's position in Britain. Albert also became unofficially Queen Victoria's principal political advisor after the uncertainty of the first years of their marriage when his role was unclear and a source of some friction between them. The Royal Children numbered nine at Princess Beatrice's birth in 1857, the succession assured. The retreat at Balmoral leased since 1848 was purchased and rebuilt to Albert's design. It provided an idyllic rural retreat, inconvenient for the Government coach carrying despatches, but loved by the Queen for the cool air, the charming cottages on the Estate, and the beautiful scenery which she sketched and which reminded Albert of his German home. State visits exchanged between Britain and her new ally France overwhelmed Victoria with the excitement and magnificence of Paris. The Crimean War which had caused grave public concern and had drawn Queen Victoria's efforts for the suffering of the troops, ended in victory. A hilltop bonfire at Balmoral at midnight celebrated the victory (unfortunately not while Lowe was present) according to Queen Victoria's Journal, "in a veritable witches' dance supported by whisky."

But the triumphs of these years were for Queen Victoria overturned in 1861 by the death of her mother, the Duchess of Kent, and then of her husband, Prince Albert. The grief and prolonged mourning meant that the Queen and Court never fully regained the lively gaiety of this decade. The Queen did not dance for eighteen years. When concerts and entertainments were resumed the court was older and more sedate, lacking the youthful brilliance and happiness of the earlier decade.

---

[5]A selection from the works of pioneer photographers in the Royal collection illustrates this edition of Lowe's Journal. The name of the photographer for each plate is given under each illustration.

For Joseph Lowe too this decade was a high point. As an established teacher he entered the Royal employ with confidence, enjoying excellent relations with the Royal Family. He was obviously popular with the children in the dancing and romping, the fishing expeditions, and the gifts and greetings taken back to the family in Edinburgh. And he enjoyed the confidence of the Queen and Prince Albert who set demanding standards for all those who educated and cared for the Royal Children. Lowe frequently writes, in these years, of the openness, kindness or "condescension" of the Queen in the lessons or encounters on walks in the country. But ill health begins to trouble Lowe, a shortness of breath prevents him dancing in 1855, and medication keeps him indoors during 1858. Some of the later journal entries are unusually terse, owing perhaps to ill health, and his last visit concludes in December 1860. He died in 1866 aged 69 years.

A fine tribute to Joseph Lowe's accomplishment as a dance master occurs in 1860 in the visit of the Prince of Wales to Canada. The heir to the throne, although slow to learn and subject to emotional outbursts at home, was the centre of public attention on the tour of Canada for his charming behaviour and stylish dancing. Some years later Prince Alfred, who had learnt the violin as well as dancing from Lowe, was in Melbourne where he provided a testimonial for Joseph's son, Joseph Eager Lowe. The Prince's Equerry wrote:

> H. R. H. The Duke of Edinburgh was instructed in Dancing for many years by Mr Joseph Lowe whose son is now settled in Melbourne, and remembers it with the greatest satisfaction.

The dancing which Lowe had taught at Court was accepted worldwide through the Empire. Together Queen Victoria and Joseph Lowe had helped reshape dancing in the English-speaking world. The Royal Family responded not only to the fresh vigour of Scottish dance but to the "most excellent master." The Princes no doubt remembered especially the successful fishing expeditions with their teacher, which the Journal allows us to glimpse, and which Joseph's Obituary in the local newspaper places alongside his pre eminent status as a dancing master:

> those who have enjoyed a day on the river side with this keen angler and genial companion will never forget his merry laugh, his quaint stories, and his indomitable buoyancy of spirit.[6]

---

[6]Obituary "The Late Mr Joseph Lowe" from The Brechin Advertiser 1866, quoted in full in the Appendix.

INTRODUCTION

The Journal

No explicit reason for writing the Journal is given by Lowe. It may have incidentally served as a log book of the lessons given, which assisted with the preparation of accounts, but its more likely purpose is the recording of the events and personalities at Balmoral and Windsor for Lowe's private record and for the interest of the family at home in Edinburgh.

That Joseph Lowe felt this was a momentous chapter of his life is evident from the Journal, and from its title written on the leather cover, "J Lowes Visits to Windsor and Balmoral since 1852." He appears to chide his daughter, who took his place for the 1856 visit, in the brief comment, "Her Journal Lost."

Later generations within the family have also felt the significance of these visits: Joseph's son in Melbourne obtained certificates and testimonials of his father's teaching from the Royal family, and the book and certificates have been carefully handed down through generations of the Lowe family (a note inserted in the cover of the Journal reads, "Please the Contents of this box to my son, J.M.Lowe"). A later young reader has marked several of the most interesting passages of the Journal with a red crayon tick.

The Journal is written in a solid-bound book 19cm x 23.5cm with marbled end papers and the same decoration on the page edges. The book which is 3 cm thick is only half filled by the 87 written pages of the Journal. Although the Journal is written in ink on both sides of the pages there is no discernible bleed-through.

The Modern Edition

In this modern edition the words written by Joseph Lowe are in plain type; all editorial additions in the text are italicised. It is however an edition for the convenience of today's reader in modernized spelling and punctuation. These alterations are numerous and are not indicated in the text. As will be seen from the facsimile pages (illustration 3) the Journal was originally written in Journal-English; it has a rapid delivery, often with the subject left out, in a string of clauses, with little punctuation. The unaltered original set in modern typescript would not have made an easily readable book, but as little as possible has been altered in this presentation, mindful of the interest of scholars in primary scripts. The main alterations are:

THE JOURNAL OF JOSEPH LOWE

1. Capital letters are standardized and altered to conform to the sentence structure. Although a certain graphic emphasis in a few phrases is thereby lost, the haphazard capitalization would have proved too distracting in a modern edition. Lowe's use of capitals for the Royal Family has been retained.

2. Spelling has been corrected and modernized. The names of some people are given in the Journal in several versions (Miss Hildyard is variously spelt Hilliard, Hillard, Heilyard by Lowe). These are corrected where the person's name can be established from another source. The Queen calls her piper "Mackay"; Lowe calls him "McKay" throughout. Even though Lowe is a Scotsman the Queen's spelling is prefered. Many proper names and the names of members of the Royal Household (listed in the Appendix) are corrected and standardized though "Welsh rabbit" is retained as Lowe spelt it.

    A few of Lowe's unconventional spellings may indicate a Scottish pronunciation, local dialect or French heritage. Spellings changed include: "breckfast," "goodby," "alittle," "excurtion," "staid" (for "stayed"), "kindely," "tour" (for "tower"), "togeather," "shortily," "posotively," "fiddeling," "emediately," "tumbeling," "dazeling," "their" (for "there"), "enterance" "untill," "freindely," "dazeling," "Nurcery" (for "Nursery"), "puple" (for "pupil"), "honor," "ugley," "hotell," "ingaged," "affraid," "affible," and very many others.

    Lowe's varied spelling is of course a positive feature of his writing, giving colour and interest to the script, but again it could not be simply transcribed into a modern print edition.

    The headings to each section of the Journal, e.g., "Mr. Lowe's First Visit to Balmoral . . . ," are retained as Lowe wrote them, with the addition of chapter numbers I–XVI. But the daily entry headings were in a variety of formats—"Sunday 23rd," "Sunday December 23," "23," "Sunday Dec 23rd"—which have all been replaced by the most common for of heading— "Sunday the 23rd."

    The Journal is tidily and fluently written throughout with very few corrections. This may indicate that Lowe actually copied into the volume from his prepared notes, as, for example, do five words crossed out on 25th September 1852 (viz "I of course stopped and") which have been written early, slightly out of context, crossed out, then copied in their correct place. This however is near the start of the Journal and copying from notes, if it occurred at all, may not have continued throughout. Several days' entries in the Journal

Third Visit to Windsor Castle to teach the Royal Children in 1854 and 1855

Left Edinr with my Daughter Charlotte on Thursday the 21st of December 1854 by the N E Railway at 8 a m for Newcastle intending to stop for the night to see Mr D'Albert's Ball, but on our arrival received an extraordinary letter from D'Albert stating that I could not be admitted, as he would not admit professional persons to see his pupils Dance, I of course felt disappointed as he and I had always been on such friendly terms, and cannot account for this piece of Caprice, We went to the Turks Head and had Dinner, then Walked out to see the Town, and Spent rather a tiresome evening, Got to the Railway station between twelve and One, and started for London at ½ past One, and arrived in London by 10 Oclock on Friday Morning, Had a Cab and drove to Webbs Hotel in Piccadilly, took off our Luggage and sent Charlotte by the Omnibus to Kensington to see Mrs

3. The Journal of Joseph Lowe, two facsimile pages: "Third Visit to Windsor Castle...1854 and 1855."

Mobson, had a jolly good Breakfast then went out to walk about, Called on Mr Muller and heard him play over a great many of his new arrangement of Reels and Strathspeys, he went with me to call for Mr Lock, Mr Lock made us go with him to Dinner to his Country House at Brompton, Had a capital Dinner and plenty of Whisky Toddy, then set to the Fiddeling of Reels and spent a very pleasent night, got back to the Hotel about Twelve and went to Bed

Saturday 23

Had Breakfast at 12 went out and called on Moncatell Saw some fine Melons then went into Lister Square and spent two Hours in the large Globe, where I saw a beautiful Model of Sebastopool and the position of all the Armies in the Country Balaklava Inkerman &c I then went to the Hotel and had some Soup, packed my portmantue and called for Charlotte at Mr Laurens in St James St and drove to the Paddington

INTRODUCTION

September 1852 (viz "I of course stopped and") which have been written early, slightly out of context, crossed out, then copied in their correct place. This however is near the start of the Journal and copying from notes, if it occurred at all, may not have continued throughout. Several days' entries in the Journal appear to have been written at one time, a fact which is sometimes recorded in the text itself. Words and headings are occasionally duplicated at page turns or elsewhere in the text. These are omitted, as are Lowe's own corrections, in this modern edition. One duplication which may be of dancing significance is the repetition of the word "turning." Lowe wrote "the great fault of the Princess Helena turning turning in her left foot" (29 September 1854). He may have meant that "the great fault of the Princess Helena *in dancing is that when* turning *she is* turning in her left foot."

In two sections of the Journal dates are incorrectly entered and at one point the name Alfred was written when the Queen's husband Albert must have been intended (24 August 1853). These errors have been corrected. When Lowe writes of Prince Ernest of Leiningen and Prince Edward of Saxe Weimar (1 January 1856) it is probable that he means Prince Charles of Leiningen and Prince Ernest of Saxe Coburg but this has not been changed.

At the end of two of his visits to Windsor, Lowe gets his landlord to "hurl" his luggage to the coach about a mile away. This interesting Scottish expression, meaning to "wheel in a cart," is replaced in the Journal after 1853 with the more conventional "take." Some older expressions like "to quiz" (meaning to tease) are also used. Modern idioms are also represented, as in the "wideawake hat" which Lady Augusta Bruce is wearing as part of her riding outfit, on 6 October 1852. This expression, which originated from a quip in Punch in 1849, described a hat made of beaver or wool felt which "had no nap" as being therefore "wideawake."

Joseph Lowe's Journal is in correct and standard English, far from his childhood Brechin dialect, and with few obvious Scottishisms. Perhaps this, and his careful writing in a substantial book, should be taken as further indications of the seriousness with which he regarded this episode of his life.

THE JOURNAL OF JOSEPH LOWE

4. The old Castle at Balmoral, 1854

At Balmoral, surrounded by the deer forests, picturesque hills and within sight of the River Dee, the Royal family spent enjoyable autumn holidays from 1848. Balmoral was a favourite residence because of the atmosphere of informality and the beautiful setting. "It was so calm, and so solitary, it did one good as one gazed around; and the pure mountain air was most refreshing. all seemed to breathe freedom and peace, and to make one forget the world and its sad turmoils"(Queen Victoria's Journal). However the medieval-style house, erected in 1830, proved too small for the Royal family and was replaced by a residence designed by Prince Albert.

Photographer: George Washington Wilson , Copyright Windsor Castle. Royal Archives.
(c) 1991. Her Majesty The Queen.

I. Mr Lowe's First Visit to Balmoral to Teach the Royal Children to Dance, September 16th 1852.

Started from Inverness on Thursday, the 16th of September by the Defiance Coach, got to Aberdeen by eight o'clock pm, called for Mrs R. Alexander, slept in McKay's Hotel. Started from Aberdeen at seven am by the Deeside Coach on Friday the 17th for Invercauld and arrived at the Inn about three pm, had some dinner, then walked back to Balmoral (about three miles) to see Colonel Phipps. Got orders from the Colonel to call at Balmoral next morning at ten o'clock to receive my orders from Her Majesty. Invercauld being so far from Balmoral, I thought it would be too far to walk every day and went in search of a lodging nearer to Balmoral. After searching about for a long time from place to place I succeeded in getting a small bedroom in one of the Forrester's Houses at Easter Balmoral within less than a mile from the Castle. I then walked back to the Inn at Invercauld and had some tea, and afterwards some toddy and went to bed.

Saturday the 18th

Had breakfast at eight o'clock, then got a cart to take my luggage to my lodgings at Easter Balmoral. After dressing, went and called for Colonel Phipps as desired. The Colonel told me that Miss Hildyard was out walking with the Royal Children and he desired me to call back in an hour. I did so and was desired to be in attendance in an hour to give my first lesson. When I returned I was shown into the Ball Room, a very large room built entirely of iron and so very hot that I could hardly breathe in it. I opened all the windows and let the fresh air blow through it. Miss Hildyard came to me first and informed me that Her Majesty the Queen and Prince Albert were to be present at the lesson. This made me feel a little nervous as I had not seen the children, nor did I know what to begin them with, as I had no idea what they could do. Miss Hildyard left and in a little she brought me in the Princess Alice, a very pretty little girl. I had fortunately time to see what Her Royal Highness could do, and got her through a few steps before the Princess Royal came in. I then took the Princess Royal, and, while I was engaged with Her Royal Highness, the Prince of Wales came in with his Tutor. The Prince came directly up to me and shook me by the hand. Prince Alfred then came in, and came up to me in the same way, with his arm extended from the shoulder, all the way up the large room. About the middle of the Princess Royal's lesson, everyone rose up and the Prince of Wales came up to me and touched me on the arm and said "Mr Lowe the Queen is coming." I of course turned round and had a most gracious bow from Her Majesty, and then went on with my lesson. Her Majesty remained

I. BALMORAL, SEPTEMBER, 1852

a long time in the room, then Prince Albert came in and came directly up to me and said that he hoped I would find them attentive pupils, and *he* tried to explain to the Prince of Wales what I meant and showed him the Step which His Royal Highness did very well indeed. When the Queen and Prince Albert retired they both made me a gracious bow. The Queen asked Miss Hildyard to express her satisfaction with the lesson and I was asked to remain for a little till Her Majesty wrote me an introduction to the Princesses of Hohenlohe who are living at Abergeldie with their Grandmother the Duchess of Kent. After finishing the lesson I was waiting in the Ball Room for the letter to Abergeldie when one of the Footmen came to me and asked me to dinner in the Stewards' Room. I had a capital dinner and just as I finished, the Queen's letter was brought to me, and after a few glasses of wine I started for Abergeldie. The Duchess of Kent and the two Princesses of Hohenlohe were out driving when I got there and I had to remain for more than an hour before they came home. I was sent for by Lady Augusta Bruce, Maid of Honour to the Princesses. Lady Augusta, being an old pupil of mine, received me most kindly, shook me by the hand, and really seemed delighted to see me. After asking all about my family & c & c Her Ladyship asked me whether it would be better for the Princesses to have their lesson by themselves or to join their cousins at Balmoral. I strongly recommended by themselves. Her Ladyship left me to go to the Duchess of Kent to give my opinion, and I was ordered to be in attendance at Abergeldie on Monday morning at ten o'clock. Her Ladyship again expressed her delight at meeting with me, shook me by the hand and bade me good-bye. I then returned to my lodgings and had tea, wrote a few letters and my advertisement for Edinburgh* then went to bed.

Sunday the 19th

Had breakfast at eight o'clock, wrote a few letters, then went to the Church of Crathie. The Queen and Prince Albert were in Church, and of course there were a great crowd to see them. After Church went and had dinner at the Castle, after dinner had a long walk with Mackay the Queen's Piper. Went to Invercauld Inn, had some toddy and got home by eight o'clock and went to bed.

Monday the 20th

Had breakfast at eight o'clock, then started for Abergeldie to give my first lesson to the Princesses of Hohenlohe. Was very kindly received by Lady Augusta Bruce *and* got the Princesses through three Scotch Steps to their

*see Illustration 7., page 31.

great delight. The snow was falling very thick. The Duchess of Kent sent many apologies for not sending a carriage for me and ordered her own carriage to the door and made them drive me direct to Balmoral. I arrived at Balmoral before one o'clock, gave a lesson to the Princess Royal and to the Princess Alice. When the lesson was over and the Princesses had gone, the Queen in a few minutes brought them back again to see what they had

5. "The Five True Positions" from *Lowes' Ball-Conductor and Assembly Guide.*

"The feet should be well turned out and pointed so as to make the toes meet the floor first; they should never be violently tossed about, or lifted high from the ground, nor should the knees be allowed to break the contour of the dress. In the ballroom, all the steps should be performed in an easy graceful manner, with minute neatness, and in rather small compass. Ladies, particularly, should rather seem to glide along with easy elegance, than strive to astonish by violent action - making their dancing appear to be a boisterous and difficult exercise. It is necessary for us, however, to warn our Pupils against falling into the opposite error of listlessness and inaccuracy, as with these elegance can never be obtained; and they must take care not to allow their dancing to become mere jolting and hobbling." (pages 6 & 7).

I. BALMORAL, SEPTEMBER, 1852

got. She expressed herself very much pleased with my style and said she should like to learn those pretty Steps herself. She took off her over-shoes and stood up before me and had a regular lesson. The Third Scotch Step of my Second Set she pronounced the most elegant Scotch Step she had ever seen and I got Her Majesty to do it very well indeed. Her Majesty then told me that Miss Seymour, her Maid of Honour, wished for a few lessons by herself. Miss Seymour remained after the Queen and the Royal Children had left and I gave her a long lesson, after which I was asked not to go away as they would all take another lesson, the day being so wet and the children not being able to take outdoor exercise. I was sent for again at four o'clock to the Dining Room, and gave my first lesson to the Princess Helena. I commenced Her Royal Highness with the Quadrille Steps. I then gave the Princess Royal and the Princess Alice another lesson, then the Prince of Wales and Prince Alfred had their lesson. When I was about to go away, the Tutor, Mr Gibbs, told me that one of the Gentlemen wished to have a lesson, and I was taken to this Gentleman's room. He is a foreign Gentleman but I did not get his name. I remained with him nearly an hour, then went to the Stewards' Room and had tea, then went home at seven o'clock, got a rousing peat fire, wrote this day's Journal then went to bed.

Tuesday the 21st

Started for Abergeldie at nine o'clock, gave a lesson *to* the Princesses of Hohenlohe, nothing particular occurred. Got to Balmoral by one o'clock, gave a lesson to the Princess Royal and to the Princess Helena, then had dinner. Was called at four o'clock and gave a lesson to the Prince of Wales and to Prince Alfred. Did not see the Queen this day, Her Majesty being out with Prince Albert on a shooting excursion. Nothing particular happened. Got home by six o'clock, wrote a letter, took it to the Post Office at Crathie, returned home, read a little then went to bed.

Wednesday the 22nd

Started for Abergeldie at nine o'clock. When about half way met the Duchess of Kent's carriage coming for me. The carriage turned and drove me right up to the Grand Entrance. Gave my lesson as usual to the Princesses of Hohenlohe and to Lady Augusta Bruce. Tried the figure of the Reel for the first time and got on very well. I then commenced them with the Elastic Expander Exercises, got through the first three Exercises very well, all seemingly quite delighted with them. Had a Message from Miss Seymour, Maid of Honour to the Queen, to be at Balmoral as soon as possible to give her a lesson. I finished the lesson at Abergeldie, and arrived at Balmoral at half past twelve. Miss Seymour was waiting for me and had a lesson by herself till one, when the Princess Royal and the Princess Alice came in with Miss Hildyard. While at their lesson a message came from the Queen, to say that Her Majesty wished them to come to dress for lunch and that Her Majesty was to return with them in half an hour. The whole party came at the appointed time, and Her Majesty took her lesson first. The Royal Children then danced their steps to Her Majesty, after which the Queen, the Prince of Wales, the Princess Royal and the Princess Alice danced a Reel. It was some time before I got them to do the Figure properly but at last we got it very well. Her Majesty then let me see several Scotch Steps she had been taught and asked if I thought them good Steps for a Lady. I told Her Majesty that I considered them much too rough and masculine, and much more adapted for Men than for Ladies. Her Majesty told me she thought so too and that she thought my Steps much more elegant and better for Ladies than anything she had seen before. When the lesson was over I went to dinner, and while at dinner Colonel Phipps sent for me to his own room and said that Her Majesty was so much pleased with me that she hoped I would find it convenient to remain till the end of the month, and asked me (from the Queen) if I could not make it convenient to come to Windsor Castle about the middle of January, in place of at Christmas. I told the Colonel that it would be very inconvenient for me at that time as it was my busiest time in all the year. I then returned to dinner and in a very short time I had another message sent to me, from Miss Seymour. I went to her, and she begged of me to give her another lesson. This engaged me till four o'clock. Then the Prince of Wales came in with his Tutor and had half an hour by himself after which I returned to my lodgings. While walking along the road, the Queen and Prince Albert drove past. I of course took off my hat, the Prince lifted his cap, Her Majesty bowed and recognised me in the most friendly manner of which I felt very proud. I got to my lodgings at five o'clock and began to write this Journal.

Thursday the 23rd

Started for Abergeldie at the usual hour and gave my lesson to the Princess in the presence of the Duchess of Kent but nothing particular ocurred. Got to Balmoral by twelve o'clock, gave Miss Seymour a lesson, then had the Royal Children. Commenced them with the Elastic Chest Expanders but nothing particular occurred, got to my lodgings by five o'clock.

Friday the 24th

Got to Abergeldie by ten o'clock, gave a lesson to the Princess Feodore and to Lady Augusta Bruce. The Princess Adelaide was confined to bed on account of having been thrown from her horse on Thursday. The Royal

I. BALMORAL, SEPTEMBER, 1852

Princesses came in during the lesson, to enquire for their cousin. They then took their lesson at Abergeldie with the Princess Feodore. I got clear by twelve o'clock and had nothing more to do that day. Went to Balmoral Castle and had dinner, then walked about the grounds all afternoon, and got home by seven o'clock.

Saturday the 25th

Got to Abergeldie at the usual hour and *gave* a lesson to the Princess Feodore and to Lady Augusta Bruce, the Princess Adelaide still being confined to her room. Got to Balmoral, gave a lesson to the Princess Royal and to the Princess Helena, then to Miss Seymour then went to dinner. In going home Her Majesty and Miss Seymour passed me on horse-back. I of course stopped and took off my hat as they passed and had a gracious bow from both of them. I got home by five o'clock.

Sunday the 26th

Very wet cold day, went to Crathie Church. The Queen did not come to Church that day. Lady Jocelyn and Miss Seymour were in the Queen's Seat. In coming out of Church I met Miss Shepherd from Edinburgh, had a chat with her, then went to Balmoral to dinner. Got home by five o'clock, then took a long walk with my Landlord nearly to Lochnagar. Got home between seven and eight. Mr Mackay, the Queen's Piper, called and we had some toddy. Got to bed by nine o'clock.

Monday the 27th

Got to Abergeldie at the usual hour, ten o'clock. In the middle of the lesson the Queen came in with the Prince of Wales and Prince Alfred which put a stop to the lesson for a short time. Her Majesty then expressed a wish to dance a Reel. The party were the Queen, Prince of Wales, the Princess Feodore of Hohenlohe and Prince Alfred. There were in the room besides, the Duchess of Kent, Prince Herman of Hohenlohe, the Princess of Hohenlohe (his mother), Lady Augusta Bruce, Lady Jocelyn and Miss Seymour besides the Governesses. Got to Balmoral by twelve o'clock, gave a lesson to *the* Princess Royal and to the Princess Alice, then to the Prince of Wales, and to Prince Alfred. Had dinner and got to my lodgings by 5 o'clock.

Tuesday the 28th

Started for Abergeldie at the usual hour. When about half way met a messenger with a note for me from Lady Augusta Bruce to say not to come to Abergeldie till twelve o'clock as Her Majesty and the Royal Children were to be at Abergeldie at that hour to have a general practising. I went home again and walked about, but arrived at Abergeldie at the appointed time and met the whole party. Her Majesty, the Prince of Wales, the Princess Feodore of Hohenlohe and Prince Alfred danced the first Reel. The Princesses then danced all their Steps. We then had the Lady of the Lake Country Dance, then Reels and Steps again. The whole party seemed quite pleased and said they had had a nice Ball. I then walked to Balmoral to dinner and got to my lodgings by five o'clock.

Wednesday the 29th

Was ordered to be at Balmoral by twelve o'clock to meet the same party I had at Abergeldie the day before. The day being very cold and wet, the carpet in the Dining Room was rolled back, and the whole party went through everything that was done the day before at Abergeldie with the addition of the Reel of Tulloch in which Her Majesty took a part and danced in the most spirited style. Her Majesty then said that she would show me some more Steps that she had learned before and asked my opinion of them. I told Her Majesty that they were truly Scotch Steps but in my opinion too rough for Ladies and more adapted for Men. Her Majesty said she was of the same opinion and that she thought my Steps much more elegant and the best for Ladies she had ever seen. Her Majesty is very quick in picking up the Steps. She said to me, "Oh Mr Lowe, it is all very easy to dance these steps to your violin, but when I come to try them in the evening to the pipes I forget every one of them." I told Her Majesty that it could not be expected that she could remember them as she had not had sufficient time for the practice to become a habit, but that I felt convinced that in a very short time Her Majesty would dance a Reel as well as any Lady in Scotland, with which compliment Her Majesty seemed quite pleased. Prince Albert was in the room a long time and seemed quite amused, and went away snapping his fingers. The whole party are to have another Dance of the same kind tomorrow. I had dinner and went home. Shortly after getting home a messenger came to me with Orders to be at the Castle again at six o'clock, as they meant to have another Dance in the evening. I went at the appointed hour but in the meantime Lord Hardinge arrived and I was sent word that they would not have more dancing that night and so I had tea at the Castle and went home.

Thursday the 30th

Got to Balmoral by twelve o'clock, was asked to the Drawing Room, met the whole party again, and had a regular practising, everything the same as the day before. I taught them the Reel of Eight. Her Majesty thought it

THE REEL OF TULLOCH.

6. The Reel of Tulloch

"It was this reel which so especially delighted Her Majesty, Queen Victoria, when on a visit to Scotland in 1842. At the Ball given by the Marquis of Breadalbane, at Taymouth Castle, the original figure of the Reel O' Thulican was danced in the Royal presence, with admirable characteristic spirit . . . The Queen seemed quite elated during the performance, and expressed herself much delighted and astonished at the lively execution displayed by the Dancers." (Footnote to "The Reel of Thulichan, The Queen's Favourite," in *The Royal Collection* . . .)

There are numerous references to the popularity of this dance and its performance at Balls and competitions. The Reel of Tulloch appears to have been composed about 1800. Its gaelic name Ruidleadh Thulichan also gave rise to the name Reel of Thulichan, which Lowe also uses. Several versions of the dance were known, some in combination with the old Foursome Reel. Its most distinctive feature was the swinging with linked arms. There was also a special method of changing direction in the middle of the swing. During the eight bar setting periods the dancers used any quick reel setting step they pleased, putting in as many different steps as possible in the course of the dance.

great fun and entered quite into the spirit of it. They all danced for an hour and a half, I then went to dinner, after dinner I was asked to the Ball Room to Miss Seymour. Colonel Gordon and the German Governess came in, and all had a long lesson. Got home by six o'clock.

Friday the 1st

Was ordered to be at Balmoral by eleven o'clock to give Miss Seymour and the German Governess a lesson. They had nearly an hour by themselves. Was then called to the Drawing Room and met the usual party, had a practising the same as on the previous days. Her Majesty, as attentive as any of them, remained with them for an hour and a half then went to dinner. Had a message from Miss Seymour and the German Governess that they wished to have another lesson for the Figure. They could not get anyone to dance with them but Mackay the Piper. He and I were the Gentlemen. Got to my lodgings by six o'clock.

Saturday the 2nd

Went and gave my lesson at Abergeldie as usual. No lesson at Balmoral this day. Wrote some letters and when taking them to the Post Office, met the Queen and Prince Albert in their carriage. Had a gracious bow from the Queen and the Prince took off his cap in returning my salute. Got home and went to bed by nine o'clock.

Sunday the 3rd

Had a tremendous long walk with my Landlord. Landed amongst the snow on the top of Lochnagar by twelve o'clock. Went down the back of the mountains, through Invercauld Deer Forest, where we saw hundreds of deer. We walked up the river side to the Bridge of Dee where we crossed the river then walked down the other side to Invercauld Inn where we had dinner, then walked home in the evening. We could not have walked less than from 30 to 40 miles.

Monday the 4th

No lesson at Abergeldie today. Got to Balmoral by half past twelve, gave a lesson to the Princess Royal, then Her Majesty came in and had a lesson, then the Princess Alice had a lesson, then the Prince of Wales and Prince Alfred, a very short lesson altogether as they were all going off somewhere. Had dinner and went home by five o'clock.

I. BALMORAL, OCTOBER, 1852

Tuesday the 5th

When about starting for Abergeldie I had a note from Lady Augusta Bruce stating that the Princesses of Hohenlohe would take their lesson with the Royal Children at Balmoral. Got to Balmoral by twelve o'clock, gave a good long lesson to the Princes and Princesses before the Queen came in. Her Majesty then joined in the Figures. Then Prince Albert came in. His Royal Highness Prince Albert, The Queen, The Prince of Wales and the Princess Adelaide of Hohenlohe danced the Reel of Tulloch. They all rested while I gave the Princess Helena her Quadrille Steps. Prince Albert then asked me to show him a few easy Steps. His Royal Highness did them very well indeed. He is the most perfect figure of a man I ever stood before, and beautifully turned for a dancer. His Royal Highness and the Queen then went out, and I finished the lesson and went to dinner. Was sent for by Miss Seymour and the German Governess, gave them a long lesson then went home.

Wednesday the 6th

Got to Abergeldie and gave my last lesson to the Princesses of Hohenlohe. Got to Balmoral by half past twelve. Gave a lesson to the Prince of Wales, to Prince Alfred, to the Princess Alice and to Miss Seymour then to the Princess Royal after the others went away. Got Her Royal Highness through three of the Irish Steps then went to dinner. Was called to Miss Seymour and the German Governess. They had engaged two of the Footmen to make partners for them in the Reel and had a regular good swing with the Footmen in the Reel of Tulloch. Lady Augusta Bruce came in and caught them in the middle of it. Her Ladyship had a tremendous laugh at them, but very soon joined them. Her Ladyship had been out riding and was dressed in a long riding habit with a wideawake hat, *and* trousers with straps under her shoes. She tucked up her riding habit, and danced capitally and made use of her riding whip in the most playful manner in going through the Reel. Her Ladyship presented me with a little book for my daughters. Colonel Phipps came in and Her Ladyship in the most polite manner recommended me to his especial notice and called me one of her oldest friends and that if he could do anything to oblige me he would be conferring a favour on her. The Colonel said that as he knew I was anxious to get home quickly he could send me to Perth with one of the special Messengers from the Home Office for which I expressed my thanks. The teaching finished and I went to my own lodgings.

Thursday the 7th

>Got to Balmoral at twelve o'clock, gave a lesson to the Princess Royal and the Princess Alice, then to Miss Seymour and to the German Governess. Bade all good-bye, this being my last lesson. Did not see any of the Princes this day, they being out with Prince Albert shooting.

Friday the 8th

>Got my portmanteau, fiddle box &c all packed, and got my landlord to hurl them to Balmoral by ten o'clock. Had an interview with Colonel Phipps, and was requested to be at Windsor Castle at Christmas. After bidding all good-bye got into the carriage at eleven o'clock, had a delightful ride through the Highlands and got to Perth by six o'clock. Got a train just starting for Edinburgh and was in my own house by nine o'clock at night accomplishing the whole distance in ten hours.

LOWE'S ROOMS, 52 FREDERICK STREET.

DANCING, CALISTHENICS, AND DEPORTMENT.

MR and the MISSES LOWE beg leave to announce that they will RE-OPEN their ACADEMY on MONDAY the 4th October.

The Classes will be conducted as formerly.

Cards of Terms and Hours of Attendance to be had at the Academy.

Boarding Schools and Private Families attended.

Balmoral Castle, Sept. 18, 1852.

7. Joseph Lowe's advertisement in *The Scotsman*, Saturday 25th September, 1852.

This is the advertisement mentioned in the Journal on the 18th September. While some dance teachers announced they were patronised by royalty, Joseph Lowe is content to append the address "Balmoral Castle" to his advertisement.

II. Mr Lowe's First Visit to Windsor Castle to Teach the Royal Family in 1852.

Started with my daughter Euphemia from Edinburgh on Friday December 24th by the North British Railway. Got to York by seven o'clock pm, nearly two hours behind time. Stopped in York for seven hours then started for London at two o'clock in the morning. Did not reach London till three o'clock in the afternoon, two hours behind the regular time. Got a cab and drove to Mrs Robson's at Kensington, had a capital dinner, left Euphemia in Mrs Robson's, and got a bed in a lodging house next door.

Sunday the 26th

Went out and had breakfast in a Coffee House then called to see Euphemia at Mrs Robson's. They all went off to Church and I went and engaged a cab to take me to the Paddington Station to be ready for the first train for Windsor. Started at twelve o'clock and got to Windsor by two, put up at the Star and Garter Hotel, had some dinner then walked out to see the Castle. Met with Mr Mackay the Piper, I took him to the Hotel and we had some toddy. I then went with him to his lodgings and had tea, came to the Hotel and wrote a note to Colonel Phipps mentioning my arrival in Windsor and that I would wait upon him in the morning. I then had a welsh rabbit and went to bed.

Monday the 27th

Got up at eight o'clock, had breakfast then called on Colonel Phipps at ten o'clock. Sent in my card and was asked to come in. In a few minutes Colonel Phipps came to me, he asked very kindly how I was and how I had been since he saw me at Balmoral. He told me that the Queen and the Royal Children had been enquiring about me and asking if he knew when I was to be at Windsor. He asked what hotel I had put up at and said he would send me my Orders in the course of the forenoon and asked me not to be out of the way. I came to the hotel immediately and am now waiting for his Messenger. The Messenger came with a note from Lady Barrington stating that there would be no lesson till tomorrow night at six o'clock. I went out in search of a lodging and got one in Mr Gibbs', one of the Footmen at the Castle. Went to the Hotel and had dinner, then got a cab and drove to my lodging. Wrote some letters, went out in the evening to the Theatre and got home by eleven o'clock.

Tuesday the 28th

Breakfasted at nine, went to take a walk. Met with Mackay in the Long Walk of Windsor Park, went with him to call for Mr McDonald, Prince Albert's Principal Man. Mr McDonald has charge of all the Fancy Dogs and has a house at the Kennels. Had some whisky and water with McDonald, he then took me through the Kennels and showed me all the dogs, some of them very uncommon, but in my eyes very ugly. Walked to the Castle with McDonald where he left me, and I went to an Eating House and had dinner. On my way home, met with a Messenger in search of me with a letter from Mr Gibbs, the Tutor to the Royal Princes, requesting me to be at the Castle at five o'clock to give the Prince of Wales and Prince Alfred a lesson. Met with Mr McDonald again. He took me into the Castle and to his own bedroom to change my shoes, leave my fiddle case &c. Sent up my card to Mr Gibbs and was asked to the Great Oak Room where I met the Prince of Wales. His Royal Highness came up to me and shook me by the hand in the most friendly manner, asking me if I did not think this a beautiful room and drew my attention to the tapestry pictures. They are the most splendid things I ever saw. His Royal Highness had a good lesson then the Governess brought me in the Princess Helena and the Princess Louise, a very beautiful little child that I had not before seen. I got her to do the Positions and the Changing, and the Princess Helena went through the Quadrille Steps that I taught her at Balmoral. Then Miss Hildyard with the Princess Royal, the Princess Alice, and the Princess Adelaide of Hohenlohe came in. They all shook hands with me, then all had a lesson, after which they, with the Prince of Wales and Prince Alfred, danced a Reel. They then asked me to let them have the Lady of the Lake Country Dance, their Balmoral favourite, with this the lesson finished. Was asked to be at the Castle at one o'clock next day to give the younger Princesses their lesson, and at a quarter before five to meet the others. Went to McDonald's room to put on my boots &c and leave my fiddle, then Mr McDonald went with me to my lodgings where we had some toddy. I played a few Reels to him, then walked back to the Castle with him where I left him, then came home to bed.

Wednesday the 29th

Breakfasted at nine then went to McDonald's and gave his boys a lesson in Exercises. Went to the Castle at one and gave a lesson to Princesses Helena and Louise. Got over the lesson before two, then went to dinner. Got home before four to dress, got to the Castle before five, gave a lesson to the Prince of Wales and to Prince Alfred. Then Miss Hildyard brought in the Princess Royal and the Princess Alice with their Expanders and

II. WINDSOR, DECEMBER, 1852

Sceptres, to have a lesson in *the* presence of Sir James Clark, their Medical Attendant. I did not know that it was Sir James Clark till after the lesson, but it was evident that he had been sent to see if he approved of the Exercises. He expressed no opinion to me but from his manner and his looks he evidently seemed pleased. The Princesses then danced their Scotch Steps which finished the lesson. Mr McDonald was waiting for me in his own room, I went with him to his house, and spent the evening. Got home by half past eleven and went to bed.

Thursday the 30th

Breakfasted at nine, wrote two letters and was in attendance at the Castle at one. Gave the Princess Helena and the Princess Louise a lesson, then went and had dinner. Went home and dressed and got to the Castle at half past four, gave the Prince of Wales and Prince Alfred their lesson. Then Miss Hildyard with the Princess Royal and the Princess Alice came in. The two Princes and the two Princesses danced a Reel, then the Reel of Tulloch. The two Princes then went away, and the Princess Royal and the Princess Alice had their regular lesson. Got done by six o'clock, went home and read a little then went and spent the evening with Mr Renwick, a genuine Scotsman.

Friday the 31st

Breakfasted at nine then went to give McDonald's boys an Exercise lesson. No lesson at the Castle this day till half past four. Went through all the Dog Kennels then down to the river side with McDonald's boys. Went and saw the Piggery, then back to Windsor to dinner. Went home to dress and meet Euphemia, who had just arrived from London, in my lodgings. Got to the Castle by half past four, gave a lesson to the Princess Royal and to the Princess Alice, then to the Prince of Wales and to Prince Alfred. They had received some beautiful boxes of chocolate fruit from Germany. They all brought their boxes to let me see them and each made me take some of the fruit from their boxes. They at the finish of the lesson shook hands with me and wished me a Happy New Year. I then left and went home to tea with Euphemia. When we were about going to bed a Messenger came from the Castle inviting me and my daughter to a Ball that was going on in the Servants' Hall. We went and were enjoying it when the Ladies and Gentlemen of the Court came in, headed by Lord Aberdeen. After sitting for a while Miss Seymour sent one of the Footmen for me, came out of her seat to meet me, and shook me heartily by the hand in presence of the whole party and asked me to introduce my daughter to her, which I did. After a little, Lady Ely sent one of the Footmen to me to ask me to dance a Country Dance with Her Ladyship which of course I did, then after I had Her Ladyship for a partner in a Reel, then in the Reel of Tulloch. Then after a few glasses of wine in Mr Renwick's room, we left and came home to bed.

Saturday the 1st

No lesson at the Castle, today being New Year's Day, breakfasted at ten then walked out with Euphemia, and hired a pianoforte from one of the Music Shops. Walked up to the Castle and went to the Kitchen to see the great Baron of Beef roasting, 270 pounds weight of it. The Kitchen is a most extraordinary sight, so many great fires, stoves, stewpans &c &c. Met Mr Baylis who was Head Cook at Balmoral, and received great attention from him. He showed us everything that was worth seeing and also took us to see the Gold Room, the most gorgeous sight I ever beheld. The value of the Gold Plate in that room is estimated at three millions of money. From thence we went to McDonald's and I gave his boys another Exercise lesson. We then went back to Windsor and had dinner in a Coffee House. Took Euphemia home then went out in search of Mr Blagrove who had come to Windsor to lead a Grand Concert in the Castle for which I had received tickets from the Prince of Wales for myself and my daughter. After a good deal of running about from hotel to hotel, I found Mr Blagrove and his two brothers, had some wine with them and took them all to my lodgings to tea. They soon left to dress for the Concert. We also dressed and went off to the Castle to hear the concert in St George's Hall, a very long narrow room, I should think from 130–140 feet long, but not more than from 50 to 60 feet wide. The Queen, Prince Albert, all the Royal Children, the Duchess of Kent, the Princes and Princesses of Hohenlohe, the Princess Mary of Cambridge and all the Nobility and the Ladies and Gentlemen of the Court were present. The Orchestra mustered upwards of 100 performers. The music was one of Mendlessohn's Oratorios, principal singer Miss L. Pine. The effect was grand in the extreme. After the Concert we were asked by Miss Cups to her room where we had a glass of wine. We then left and got home by twelve o'clock.

Queen Victoria records in her Journal for the 1st January 1853 :

"We had a concert in St George's Hall, consisting of selections from Mendelssohn's compositions, beginning with the "Hymn of Praise." The other parts were from "Christus"(An oratorio, with only a few Choruses) & the "Lorlei"(an unfinished opera) both, posthumous works. It was a most excellent performance. "Christus" struck me as peculiarly beautiful, though all were so fine. The Orchestra was formed from my Private Band, with additions from the Philharmonic Society & Royal

II. WINDSOR, JANUARY, 1853

Opera. The Chorus, 60 in number, were from the Sacred Harmonic Society, Exeter Hall. The solo singers were Miss Louisa Pyne, Miss M. Williams, Mr Lockey, Mr Whitehouse, & Mr Lawler. The whole was under the direction of Mr Anderson."

The programme for this "Grand Performance of Mendelssohn's Works" is held in the Royal Collection in the Music Room, The British Library.

Sunday the 2nd

A very wet rainy day, had to keep the house till four o'clock. We then went to St George's Chapel in Windsor Castle and heard a very beautiful musical performance. Came home, had tea then read for a while and went to bed.

Monday the 3rd

Breakfasted at nine, then went out about the piano, then went and gave McDonald's boys their lesson. Then to the Castle to give the Princess Helena and the Princess Louise their lesson. Got home to dinner before three, had a walk with my daughter then went to the Castle at half past four to give the other Princesses and Princes their lesson. Her Majesty came into the room and asked me several questions about the children. Prince Albert also came in and asked me "How do you do Mr Lowe." I gave Miss Hildyard the sheets of the Country Dance music and she promised to use her influence to get me permission to dedicate the work to the Princess Royal, and also to use her influence to get my daughter introduced to the Royal Family. After finishing the lesson I came home, then went with my daughter to spend the evening with Mrs McDonald. Spent a very happy evening and got home by twelve o'clock.

Tuesday the 4th

Breakfasted at nine. Mr Mackay the Piper called, Euphemia and I played a number of Reels to him. I went to the Castle at one and gave the younger Princesses their lesson. Miss Hildyard came and asked me to be back at five

---

(Opposite) The Princess Royal and Princess Alice, just over two years apart in age, often shared their Dance lessons with Mr Lowe. They were close companions as children though the quieter Alice suffered from the comparison with her outgoing and intelligent older sister. In the Dance lessons it is the daring and lively Princess Royal who has a fall, but the conscientious Princess Alice, perhaps the most talented dancer of the Royal Children, who learns the character dance the Spanish Guaracha.

8. The Princess Royal and Princess Alice, 1855

Photographer: Roger Fenton. Copyright Windsor Castle. Royal Archives. (c) 1991. Her Majesty The Queen.

II. WINDSOR, JANUARY, 1853

and to bring my daughter with me. I went home with the good news to Euphemia and had dinner, dressed and got to the Castle with my daughter at five. The Prince of Wales came in first and had his lesson then Miss Hildyard came in with the Princess Royal and the Princess Alice. They both went up to Euphemia and shook hands with her. We then began the Exercises lesson with Euphemia standing before them. In the middle of the lesson the Queen came in with Prince Albert and Baron Stockmar. They all remained during the lesson and in going away Her Majesty expressed herself very much pleased with my daughter. The Princess Royal then wished to dance with Euphy and had her for a partner in the Lady of the Lake Country Dance and afterward in a Quadrille. Then the lesson finished, they shook hands with us both, and the Princess Royal expressed a hope that she would see my daughter every day. We then came home and had tea wrote some letters then went to bed.

Wednesday the 5th

Breakfasted at nine then went out and gave McDonald's boys their lesson. Got to the Castle at one, and gave the younger Princesses their lesson. Came home and had dinner, then returned to the Castle with Euphemia at half past four. Gave the Princess Royal and Princess Alice a lesson in Exercises, Euphemia showing them and I playing. Then gave the Prince of Wales and Prince Alfred their lesson. Got over before six then went home and dressed for an evening party at Mr Renwick's. Spent a very happy night got home at three in the morning.

Thursday the 6th

No lesson at the Castle today it being Twelfth Day. Went with Mr Cowlie and saw the Horse Guards Barracks, then went and gave McDonald's boys their lesson. Went with the boys to fish in the Thames, a very cold wet day, got nothing. Got home by four o'clock, had tea, then went with Euphemia to see the Queen's Table, set out for dinner. The quantity of gold plate was quite dazzling and altogether it was the most magnificent sight we ever saw. And we were then taken to the Confectioner's Room to see the Twelfth Cake *but* I did not think so much of it. We then went to Mr McDonald's room for a little, then went home to bed.

Friday the 7th

Breakfasted at nine. Mackay called and we played some Reels to him. I then went and gave the younger Princesses their lesson at the Castle at one. Came home and had dinner, dressed and got back to the Castle by four. Saw all the younger children at the Nursery window, Euphemia of course very anxious to see them. They were making play with me, holding up their different toys to the window to let me see them. Her Majesty and the Princess Mary of Cambridge came to the window. We of course drew back, but in a few minutes the whole of them were brought into the room where we were, "to shake hands with Miss Lowe" as the Governess said. Little Prince Arthur asked me to play God Save the Queen, to which he listened most attentively. I then played The Pigs' March to him with which he seemed very much delighted. They were then taken away and the elder Princesses and Princes came and had a long lesson. It being the last, they all shook hands and bade us good-bye. Her Majesty sent us tickets for the Theatrical Performance that was to take place this evening. We went home and had tea then back again to the Castle to see the play. The piece was the second part of King Henry the Fourth. Phelps acted the part of the King and Bartley the part of Sir John Falstaff. All the other parts were filled up by the best London men. The scenery was very fine and everything seemed perfect. The Queen, Prince Albert, all the Royal Children, the Duchess of Kent, Princess Mary of Cambridge, the Prince of Leiningen, Prince and Princesses of Hohenlohe and all the Nobility at Court were present as also all the Nobility and Gentry in the surrounding country. The sight was grand in the extreme. Had some wine in Miss Cup's room then went home.

Saturday the 8th

Packed up all our boxes and started for London, on our way home at quarter past ten. Arrived in London between eleven and twelve, got a cab and drove to Euston Station and left our trunks. Then went out and purchased several presents for the family at home. Dined in Hungerford Market, got to Euston Sqr by eight o'clock and started for Edinburgh a quarter before nine. Got to Edinburgh by one o'clock on Sunday forenoon, where we found all well and all expecting us. The whole trip has been most pleasant and highly gratifying.

III. Second Visit to Balmoral to Teach the Royal Children in 1853

Finished the Northern Meeting Ball on the 16th of September at half past five o'clock. On the seventeenth got my trunks packed and was on the top of the coach for Aberdeen at seven *am and* arrived in Aberdeen at seven pm. Secured places for my son John and myself by the Ballater Coach on the Sunday morning. Had some refreshment then went and called for Mrs Alexander and then went to the hotel to bed. Started next morning for Ballater at seven, arrived at Balmoral by three o'clock on the 18th September, everyone very glad to see me. Had some tea then went out to walk. Had a very long walk with John and Sandy McDonald and, while passing through the woods of Abergeldie, the Queen and Prince Albert drove past in their carriage. Her Majesty recognised me at once and said over the side of the carriage "How do you do Mr Lowe." Her Majesty seemed to take great notice of my boy and looked over the back of the carriage at him for some time. The Prince also looked back. We got home to our lodging at seven o'clock and learned that the Queen in passing my lodging saw McDonald's children playing with some toys that I brought to them. Her Majesty stopped the carriage and asked the little girl who gave her that nice doll. The child said at once that it was Mr Lowe. Her Majesty said "Was it not very kind of Mr Lowe to bring you such a nice doll?" and then passed on.

Monday the 19th

Went to the Castle at eleven to get my Orders and was asked to be in attendance at one. Went to my lodgings for my fiddle and got to the Castle at the time appointed. The Prince of Wales was first brought to me, His Royal Highness was very glad to see me and shook hands with me in the most kind way possible. His Royal Highness had a lesson, and Miss Bulteel, Maid of Honour to the Queen, then had a lesson. Prince Alfred then came and was equally glad to see me. After the lesson Mr Gibbs, the Tutor, told me that Prince Alfred had had some Fiddle lessons from Mr Anderson in London and asked me to hear His Royal Highness play. But as we were commencing the fiddling the Princess Royal came in for her dancing lesson, and the fiddling was stopped. I made arrangements to hear Prince Alfred at four o'clock. I put his fiddle in order but something came in the way and Prince Alfred could not come at the time appointed. The Princess Alice then came in and the two Princesses had a Dancing lesson. They remembered all their Scotch Steps very well indeed and some of the Irish Steps. They asked me why I did not bring my little boy. I asked them how they knew that I had a little boy with me. They said that their Mamma had told them, and they asked me to be sure to bring him with me to the Castle tomorrow. After finishing their lesson, Mr Gibbs, the Tutor, had a lesson. I then went and inspected the new building and got home to my lodging at five o'clock. Met Mr Miller the House Steward, took him into my lodging and had some grog with him. Mackay the Piper then called with another gentleman and we had tea. Johnnie told me that in the afternoon when the two Princes were passing the lodgings, the Prince of Wales called out to him "How do you do Master Lowe." Mrs McDonald told me that Johnnie very politely took off his bonnet and made a bow to the Prince. This night I began Johnnie to the fiddle. We went to bed at nine o'clock. Just as I had got into bed a knocking came to the door by one of the grooms with a horse, with Orders for me to come to the Castle immediately. I got up and was dressed just as another groom came to say that I would not be required that night so I turned into bed again.

Tuesday the 20th

Got to the Castle at eleven o'clock and gave Prince Alfred a Fiddle lesson. I was surprised how well the child understood what he was about. He played God Save the Queen by heart and several other simple airs. He promises to be a first-rate player, his musical ear is so very good. The Prince of Wales then came in with the Tutor and the two Princes had their Dancing lesson. Then the Princess Royal and the Princess Alice came and had their lesson. I got done with them all by three o'clock. After dinner I had a long walk with Johnnie and Mr McDonald. We crossed the river at the Bridge of Crathie, walked up the opposite side of the river and recrossed at the blacksmith's in a boat, and down the Balmoral side of the river where we met the Prince of Wales, Prince Alfred, Mr Gibbs and Mackay, fishing. They had not caught anything and they asked me to try. I did so and caught only one trout. I had hold of several others but they wriggled off as Prince Alfred was pulling them in, very much to his disappointment. Went home, had some tea, Willie Blair called, I had a tune with him, then got to bed by ten o'clock.

Wednesday the 21st

Got to the Castle by eleven o'clock and gave Prince Alfred a Fiddle lesson. Then the Prince of Wales came, and the two Princes had their Dancing lesson after which Mr Gibbs had a lesson, Her Majesty and the Princesses having gone to Lochnagar. I did not see any of them this day. Got home by four o'clock. Made a kite for Johnnie, wrote a few letters, then to bed by ten o'clock.

28

PRINCE ALFRED'S. Reel. By Jos. Lowe.

9. Prince Alfred, 1854

Prince Alfred, the fourth of the Royal Children, though often involved in reckless outdoor pursuits was considered to be intelligent, enquiring and hard working. Lowe found Alfred a talented musician in the violin lessons, and in later life Alfred was President of the Royal Albert Hall Amateur Orchestral Society of which Sir Arthur Sullivan was conductor.

As a child Alfred was promised as heir to his father's family and he became Duke of Saxe-Coburg in 1893, but his passion was for the sea; he joined the Navy in 1858 aged 14 years.

Photographer: Roger Fenton. Copyright Windsor Castle. Royal Archives. (c) 1991. Her Majesty The Queen.

Thursday the 22nd

Got to Balmoral by eleven and gave Prince Alfred a Fiddle lesson. The Prince of Wales and Prince Alfred then had a Dancing lesson, the Princess Royal and the Princess Alice then came and had their lesson, then Mr Gibbs had a lesson. I got home by five o'clock. Lady Augusta Bruce was at the Merchants and sent for me to kindly enquire after the welfare of myself and family. I had a long chat with Her Ladyship. She seemed very much pleased to meet with me again. Went home, gave Johnnie his fiddle lesson, and got to bed by ten.

Friday the 23rd

No lesson at the Castle this day, Her Majesty having gone to Altusuch and the children were spending the day somewhere in the neighbourhood. I went across the hills to fish on the River Muik. It turned out a very bad day of snow, sleet and rain. I however tried for a short time and caught 18 small trout. My guide W Blair got into a farmhouse with some of the gillies and got himself quite spoiled which spoiled all my day's sport. We scrambled all down the river side over the rocks and landed after a long walk in Ballater. I had to hire a gig to take him home. We got home by nine o'clock, tired enough, and I got to bed immediately.

Saturday the 24th

Got to the Castle at eleven and gave Prince Alfred his Fiddle lesson. The Prince of Wales, the Princess Royal and the Princess Alice then came and after their Steps and Expander exercises they all danced a Reel, then the Reel of Thulichan. The Princess Royal got a dreadful fall and skinned her elbow. She did not cry but her eyes filled with tears. Prince Albert looked in during the lesson and said "How do you do Mr Lowe." Gave Mr Gibbs a lesson after them, went home to Johnnie for his fiddle, and got to bed by ten o'clock.

Sunday the 25th

Very wet cold day, went to the Church of Crathie to hear Dr Robt Lee preach, Her Majesty, the Prince, and Miss Bulteel in the Royal Gallery. The Doctor preached from Romans 8th and 24th (But We are Saved by Hope &c &c). He gave *a* beautiful sermon which seemed to please the Royal Party very much. They were not very sure if it was Dr Lee that was preaching and Colonel Gordon sent Mackay the Piper round to me to know positively if it was Dr Lee. I told them that it was and that I was a hearer of his in Edinburgh so that there could be no mistake. I then went to the Castle to

III. BALMORAL, SEPTEMBER–OCTOBER, 1853

dinner, then came home to my lodging, had a glass of toddy with Mackay, wrote two letters and went to bed.

Monday the 26th

Got to the Castle by eleven, the Princes being out with Her Majesty did not do anything till one. I then had the Princess Royal and the Princess Alice and gave them a lesson. Then I gave the Princess Helena a lesson and went to dinner. After dinner gave Miss Bulteel a lesson. In the course of her lesson all the Princesses came in and they had some Reels and the Reel of Thulichan. On my way home I met with the Princess Royal and the Princess Alice with the French Governess on their ponies and walked beside them chatting and laughing all the way till I came to my lodgings. The Princess Royal then asked to see Johnnie, I went into the lodgings to bring him out. They asked him to be sure to come to the Castle tomorrow, which he promised to do by a blunt "Yes."

Tuesday the 27th

Got to the Castle as usual by eleven o'clock to give Prince Alfred his fiddle lesson and took Johnnie with me. The Queen and the Prince Albert came in to hear Prince Alfred play and expressed themselves very much pleased. Prince Alfred and I played first and second and Prince Albert sung a bass very prettily indeed. Her Majesty asked Johnnie how he was and said to me that she heard that he was delicate but said no boy could look in more robust health. I told Her Majesty that he was perfectly well. She asked me how the dancing was going on and said that she intended to have some lessons herself again but that she had fallen and hurt her knee and must defer it for a day or two. After they left, the Prince of Wales came and had a lesson, he and Johnnie danced together all the time. They had the Lady of the Lake Step, then Petronella, then the Waltz and Polka, Johnnie dancing as Lady to the Prince of Wales. Prince Alfred then came in and went through the same course with Johnnie, the Princess Royal and the Princess Alice then came and had their lesson after which I went to dinner. Was sent for by Miss Bulteel. Her Majesty and Prince Albert came into the room while I was teaching Miss Bulteel but did not remain. I finished and went home by five o'clock, had some fiddling with Willy Blair, wrote a letter then went to bed.

Wednesday the 28th

Got to the Castle by eleven o'clock and gave Prince Alfred his Fiddle lesson. Then had the Prince of Wales and Prince Alfred for their Dancing Lesson. Then was called to the Princess Royal's room to give Her Royal Highness and the Princess Alice a lesson in Calisthenic Exercises. This was the day appointed for laying the Foundation Stone of the Principal Tower of the new Castle. All the people on the Estate were invited to witness the ceremony. The hour appointed was three o'clock and by that time a great crowd had collected all in their best attire. Exactly at half past three the Royal Party came out, led by Mackay the Piper playing The Bonny Braes

10. The new Balmoral Castle, from the opposite side of the River Dee, 1857

Queen Victoria records that as they entered the newly built castle, completed in 1856, "an old shoe was thrown after us into the house, for good luck." Joseph Lowe's account is of the celebrations for the laying of the Foundation stone of the principal tower of the new castle, in 1853, which concluded with a Ball in the evening.

The residence continued to be Victoria's favourite: "It is not alone the pure air, the quiet and beautiful scenery, which makes it so delightful—it is the atmosphere of loving affection and the hearty attachment of the people around Balmoral which warms the heart and does one good." Here the Queen's love of Scotland could be given free reign: in the tartan carpets and other furnishings of the new house, the new cottages, school and library for the tenants on the estate, and riding through the hills, walks and sketching.

Photographer: George Washington Wilson. Copyright Windsor Castle. Royal Archives.
(c) 1991. Her Majesty The Queen.

III. BALMORAL, SEPTEMBER, 1853

O Mar. Then Her Majesty and the Duchess of Kent on each arm of Prince Albert, then all the Royal Children followed by the Ladies and Gentlemen of the Court. The stone was suspended by a windlass above where it was to be laid, and when all the party were on the platform, the Minister of Crathie gave an impressive prayer. The Queen then deposited a tin canister containing the different coins, newspapers, &c and a parchment written out for the occasion with the signatures of all the Royal Family. The hole in the stone wherein this canister was deposited was then filled up with cement and an iron cover put over all. The whole surface of the lower stone was then covered with lime, Her Majesty giving the finishing strokes with a silver trowel. The suspended stone was then lowered slowly down and placed on the top of the other. When in its place the square was handed to Her Majesty who applied it to the stone, then the level was laid upon it. Her Majesty then emptied the Horn of Plenty over it, then poured some oil and wine. Her Majesty then got a gilded hammer and gave the stone a few beats. The Master Mason then stood up on a high stone and waved his hat. The whole people then gave three cheers which completed the ceremony. The Royal Party then returned to the Castle in the same order as they came out. All the workman employed at the new building then went to the Iron Ball Room where an excellent dinner was prepared for them. After dinner, until the room was cleared for the Ball, the young workmen went out to the green and entered into all kinds of games such as tossing the caber, throwing the hammer, & c. The Ball Room being cleared by seven o'clock, a great many came with their wives and sweethearts and the Ball began in earnest to inspiring strains of Willie Blair's band. About eight o'clock the Queen, the Prince, the Duchess of Kent, all the Royal Children and the Ladies and Gentlemen of the Court came into the Ball Room and remained on a platform raised for them for about an hour, the Reels and nothing but Reels going on fast and furious which Her Majesty and all the Royal Party seemed to enjoy exceedingly. Shortly after the Royal Party left I went home. The Ball was kept up with great spirit till nearly twelve o'clock when all dispersed, very much pleased with the exceeding kindness and condescension of their Royal Hostess.

Thursday the 29th

Got to the Castle at eleven and gave Prince Alfred his fiddle lesson. I then had the Prince of Wales for his dancing lesson then the Princess Royal and Prince Alfred for their dancing lesson. The Princess Alice was out with the Queen and had no lesson this day. I went to dinner and had nothing more to do. Got to my lodgings by four o'clock, gave Johnnie a fiddle lesson, read a while, wrote some letters then went to bed.

Friday the 30th

Gave the Prince of Wales and Prince Alfred their usual lesson but had not any of the Princesses this day they being out riding with the Queen. Johnnie danced all the time with the Princes and also danced his Highland Fling to Miss Hildyard. I got home by four o'clock.

Saturday the 1st

Went to the Castle early to see Colonel Phipps to enquire about getting home. Saw the Colonel and solicited him to ask Her Majesty to allow me to get away on the following day. The Colonel told me that he would see Her Majesty at lunchtime and that he would send for me to let me know. I then went and gave Prince Alfred his Fiddle lesson after which the Prince of Wales had his Dancing lesson. His Royal Highness danced all the time with my Johnnie. Miss Hildyard then brought me the Princess Royal and the Princess Alice. In a short time one of the Pages came and told us that Her Majesty was coming and in a very few minutes Her Majesty was announced. Her Majesty told me that she had forgotten some of the Steps that I had taught her and that she wished to go over them again which she did with great spirit and took a capital lesson. The Princesses then danced to Her Majesty. Her Majesty then asked to see my little boy dance his Highland Fling and Her Majesty expressed herself very much pleased. The Royal Party then went away and I went to dinner. While at dinner Colonel Phipps sent for me and told me that he had mentioned my request to the Queen and that Her Majesty had no objections to let me go, and the Colonel offered me a seat in the special Messengers' Carriage to Perth on the following morning. I then went back to finish my dinner and wine. In a short time Mr Gibbs the Tutor sent for me to see if I would go out to fish with the Princes which of course I felt very happy to do. The Prince of Wales and Prince Alfred asked me if I would go for my son Johnnie which I did. He was not at home and I had to run nearly three miles in search of him and found him playing with McDonald's children on the opposite side of the river. We made all haste to the Castle and found the Princes and Mr Gibbs waiting for us. The Princes had a dispute who should have me to fish with them. Prince Alfred got me and the Prince of Wales got Mackay the Piper and off we started for the Gelder, a small stream about two miles from Balmoral. When at the river and all ready the Princes began to fish with great enthusiasm but very soon tired of it as the river was much too small and no trout to be had. I then got Prince Alfred's rod and Mackay got the Prince of Wales'. The evening was very cold and the stream very clear and I only managed to kill three trout, Mackay got none. The three were however considered a victory by Prince Alfred over his brother. During the

11. The Prince of Wales and Prince Alfred, 1855

Photographer: J.J.E. Mayall. Copyright Windsor Castle. Royal Archives. (c) 1991. Her Majesty The Queen.

time we were fishing the Princes and my son entered into all kinds of fun and got themselves quite heated. On our way home Prince Albert rode up to us in returning from deer stalking. His Royal Highness entered freely into conversation and told us that he had just shot a fine stag after stalking him for six hours. We heard the report of both barrels not far from us. The Prince rode on and we all walked to the Castle. The Princes shook hands with Johnnie and I, and we bade Mr Gibbs goodbye. The Princes said that they should try to see us in the morning to say goodbye before we left with the Messenger. Johnnie and I went to our lodgings and packed up our trunks and went to bed.

Sunday the 2nd

After breakfast got Sandy McDonald to hurl my trunks to the Castle. We got it all packed in the Messengers' Carriage then went up to the Castle to bid some of my friends goodbye. As we came round the end of the stables we saw the Queen and all the Royal Children walking between us and the Castle. I wished to draw back but the Children observed us and they and Her Majesty came directly up the path we had to go. The Children seemed quite delighted to see us and Her Majesty very condescendingly entered very freely into conversation with me. Her Majesty feared we should feel it very cold crossing the hills and hoped that I had John well wrapped up, hoped we should get safe home, &c &c &c. The Children then all shook hands with us and hoped to see me at Windsor at Christmas &c then left us. We then went up to the Castle to say goodbye to some of my friends. We got into the Messengers' Carriage at eleven and after a very cold ride over the hills by the Spittal of Glenshee we got to Perth by six o'clock. No train to Edinburgh that night. Slept in Perth that night and started by the first train in the morning, at half past six, and arrived in Edinburgh at ten, and found all well.

(Opposite) Prince Alfred was considered a good influence on his older brother, the Prince of Wales who was subject to violent tantrums and resisted the efforts of his tutors. The future King Edward VII was given a demanding regime of study to which he was completely unsuited. It is noteworthy that Joseph Lowe (perhaps alone among the tutors) never reports any difficulties with the Prince of Wales. The fishing expeditions and the physical nature of the Exercise and Dancing lessons which Lowe could provide may have been exactly what the young boy needed.

IV. Second Visit to Windsor Castle to Teach the Royal Children Dancing and Calisthenic Exercises in 1853

Left Edinburgh with my daughter Charlotte by the nine pm train of the North British Railway to join the Great Northern at York on the 22nd of December. We got into a First Class carriage and had not to change the carriage all the way and arrived in London very comfortably by ten o'clock next morning. Got a cab and sent Charlotte on to Kensington to Mrs Robson's but stayed to do some business in London by myself till three. Then went to meet Charlotte, to dinner at Mrs Robson's at four. Had a good dinner, plenty of wine and spent a very pleasant evening and got *to* bed by ten o'clock. Breakfasted at Mrs Robson's next morning, got a cab and drove to the Windsor Station. Started *by* train for Windsor a quarter before twelve. Got to Windsor by one, hired a cab and drove to my lodgings, 5 Gloucester Place. Had some dinner then wrote to Colonel Phipps announcing my arrival and stating my intention to call upon him on Monday morning. Went out with Charlotte and hired a pianoforte then came home, had tea and went to bed.

Sunday the 25th

Breakfasted at ten then went to hear the service in St George's Chapel. Came home and dined with Mrs Gibbs at two o'clock. After dinner had a long walk with Charlotte and called upon Mrs McDonald in the Home Park. Got home to tea at half past five, after tea wrote so much of this Journal and went to bed by ten o'clock.

Monday the 26th

Breakfasted at nine then went to the Castle to see Colonel Phipps. Saw the Colonel *who* asked one of the Queen's Maids to tell Her Majesty that Mr Lowe was here. The Maid said "Her Majesty aint at home yet Sir." The Colonel then told one of the Footmen to inform Lady Barrington that Mr Lowe was here. The Footman came back and asked me to wait till Miss Hildyard and the children came in from their morning walk. I waited for half an hour. When Miss Hildyard sent for me she shook hands with me and received me very kindly. She told me that it was a holiday, but that the children were very anxious to have a lesson. I told Miss Hildyard that my eldest daughter was with me, and asked if I might bring her with me to give the lesson, and got Orders to be at the Castle at five o'clock. We got there at the hour appointed and were shown to the Red Drawing Room when, after waiting for a long time, the French Governess brought in the Princess Helena and the Princess Louise. Charlotte took the Princess Louise to the end of the room and gave her her first lesson and taught her the first Exercise and I taught the Princess Helena some of the Scotch Steps. Miss Hildyard then brought in the Princess Royal and the Princess Alice. They seemed delighted to see us both and shook hands with us very cordially. They had a lesson in the Scotch Steps also, then Mr Gibbs brought in the Prince of Wales and Prince Alfred who also seemed very glad to see me. The whole group had an Exercise lesson, they then all danced a Reel. Prince Alfred then tried his Draw the Sword Scotland, then he and the Prince of Wales danced the Highland Fling, they then all together danced the Reel of Tulloch and went away. We got Orders to be at the Castle at five o'clock on the morrow. We then got home to tea at seven, wrote a letter and went to bed at eleven.

Tuesday the 27th

Breakfasted at ten and went out to walk. Got to the Castle at five, gave all the children their usual lesson but nothing particular occurred except that Prince Albert came into the room and saw the Exercise lesson. His Royal Highness gave us both a most gentlemanly bow but did not speak to me or anyone. We got home by seven had tea and got to bed by eleven.

Wednesday the 28th

Breakfasted at ten. A message came from the Castle by one of the Footmen asking us to be at the Castle at one to give the Princesses Helena and Louise a lesson. We were there at the time appointed and gave them a long lesson. Afterwards called on Mrs Jack in the Round Tower. Got home to dinner by three then dressed and went to the Castle at five. Miss Hildyard then brought the Princess Alice and told us that Her Majesty was coming to have a lesson. The Princess Alice had a lesson in Exercises and in the Scotch Steps. Her Majesty came in and graciously bowed to us both. Her Majesty then said to me that she wished to be put in mind of the Steps that she got at Balmoral. She took off her shawl and had a long lesson. Her Majesty then asked me if my daughter would have the kindness to show her the Steps. Charlotte danced them very nicely and seemed to have pleased Her Majesty very much. Her Majesty then wished to dance a Reel with the Prince of Wales, Prince Alfred and the Princess Alice which they did with great spirit. Her Majesty then sent for the Princess Helena and the Princess Louise to see their Exercise lesson. When they came in I put up all the five beside each other and they all went through the Exercises together (The Princess Royal was not present). They then danced the Lady of the Lake Country Dance and Gayities and Gravities. Charlotte danced with Prince Alfred and the Prince of Wales with the Princess Alice. Her Majesty then

12. Queen Victoria, 1855

"Her Majesty then said to me that she wished to be put in mind of the Steps that she got at Balmoral. She took off her shawl and had a long lesson."

The Journal of Joseph Lowe, 28th December 1853.

Photographer: J.J.E.Mayall. Copyright Windsor Castle. Royal Archives. (c) 1991. Her Majesty The Queen.

left, the Princes then danced their Steps, then all left and we got home by seven o'clock to tea, wrote and read a little, and went to bed at eleven.

Thursday the 29th

Breakfasted at ten. On our way to the Castle to give the younger Princesses their lesson we met a Messenger coming to tell us that the younger Princesses could not take a lesson this morning. We went and had a long walk by Eton College and down the river side and got home to dinner by three o'clock. After dinner we dressed for the evening lesson *and* got to the Castle at five. Her Majesty came and had a lesson, the Princess Alice, the Prince of Wales and Prince Alfred had a lesson also and after dancing a Reel and the Reel of Tulloch the Queen left, and left us to finish the lesson with the children, which ended every soon after. When putting on our things Mr Gibbs the Sergeant Footman called and invited us to a Ball amongst the servants in the Great Hall. Charlotte did not go but I went up to the Castle at ten o'clock and remained at the Ball till twelve. Colonel Biddulph, Miss Bulteel and Miss Kerr, two of the Ladies in Waiting, came to the Ball with several others from the Queen's Table and remained for a long time and danced amongst the servants with great spirit. I got home by half past twelve and went to bed.

Friday the 30th

Breakfasted at ten. Mr McDonald's boys, Mr Gibbs' girl and boy, and Mackay's boy came and had a lesson at my lodging. We got to the Castle by one and had the Princess Helena and the Princess Louise for about half an hour. We then took a walk and went home to dinner at three. We then dressed and returned to the Castle at five, had a large party including Her Majesty, the whole of the Royal Children, Miss Bulteel, Miss Kerr, Miss Hildyard, Mr Gibbs &c. The whole *group* joined. They danced some Reels and two Country Dances, Her Majesty enjoying it as much as any of them and felt no hesitation in taking Charlotte's hand in going round. Her Majesty also asked Charlotte to dance in the same Reel with her on the Gentleman's side so as she might see the Steps. After the Queen left there was nothing but romping and fun as they called it, the children all striving who should get Charlotte to dance with them and she had to dance with every one. As the children were leaving Miss Kerr asked me if I had any engagement just now as she wished very much to try the Waltz. Miss Bulteel and she tried it a little together but neither of them very good at it and Charlotte had to give each of them a turn. We got home at half past seven, had tea, amused ourselves till nearly eleven, then went to bed.

III. BALMORAL, SEPTEMBER, 1853

Saturday the 31st

Got to the Castle at one and gave the younger Princesses their lesson. Took a long walk and got home to dinner at three, dressed and got back to the Castle at five. Gave the usual lesson but nothing particular occurred, got home by seven and had tea, played some music and got to bed at eleven.

Sunday the 1st

Very snowy day and did not go to Church. Went and dined with Mackay, had a very fine roasted pig *and* plenty of toddy. We then went to the Home Park and had tea with Mrs McDonald, got home through very deep snow by nine o'clock, read a little, then went to bed.

13. Princess Louise and Princess Helena, 1859.

Like all the Royal Children the sisters Louise and Helena learnt music, and how to ride, skate, swim and dance, to speak German and French, and a range of suitable subjects. But for Louise drawing and painting were her passion. Later in life she was allowed to attend lessons at the National Art Training School which Prince Albert, a patron and collector of the arts, had founded. Helena, whose favourite home was Balmoral, had a passion for riding and the outdoors.

Photographer: Caldesi. Copyright Windsor Castle. Royal Archives. (c) 1991. Her Majesty The Queen.

Monday, the 2nd

Got to the Castle by one and gave the younger Princesses their lesson. While we were engaged with them Miss Hildyard, the Princess Royal and the Princess Alice came through the room. They told us that they had all been on the ice, skating. The Princesses looked quite rosy and the perfect pictures of blooming health. Sometime after, a party of Ladies passed through the room. This morning the Princess Helena gave Charlotte a box of sweets with a gilded steam engine on the top of it. We got home to dinner by three o'clock then dressed and got back to the Castle at five. Dr Becker, the Prince of Wales and Prince Alfred were in the room waiting for us. They had a short lesson in the Club Exercises. Then Miss Hildyard brought in the Princess Royal and the Princess Alice. They all danced a Reel then the Reel of Tulloch, some Waltzing, then went away. We then called upon Mrs Jack in the Round Tower and got home for tea at eight o'clock, and to bed by eleven.

Tuesday the 3rd

Got to the Castle at one and gave the usual lesson to the younger Princesses. Got home to dinner at three, dressed and back to the Castle at half past five. We had all the Children to let the younger Princesses try a Country Dance. They danced Pop Goes the Weasel and some Reels. The Princess Royal told Charlotte that they were making up a parcel for her to take to her sisters in Edinburgh. We got home by seven, had tea, played some music and went to bed at eleven.

Wednesday the 4th

While at Breakfast a messenger came to say that we were wanted at the Castle by eleven. We got there at the hour and had all the Princesses for a short time, they were in a hurry as they were all going out on a sledge with Her Majesty. We were asked to stay till one o'clock to give the Princess Louise a lesson by herself but after waiting for a long time, a messenger came to say that the Queen had taken the Princess Louise with her, and that there would be no more dancing till six. Mr McDonald took us to show us through the Castle. We saw all the principal sights, the Gold Room, the Silver Room, the China Room, St George's Hall, the Armoury, the different State Rooms, the South and the North Corridors, the Kitchen, the Store Rooms, and almost everything. Mr Roberts, the Gentleman who has charge of all the valuable property in the Castle, spent nearly an hour with us explaining the great value of many things in the North Corridor. This corridor is never shown except by special order by Prince Albert and it was only through the kindness of Mr Roberts who keeps the keys that we got

IV. WINDSOR, JANUARY, 1854

a sight of it. We got home to dinner at half past three then dressed for the evening lesson. We got to the Castle at six and had all the children. They danced their Country Dances and some Reels. This evening they made Charlotte a number of little presents, small toys, boxes of sweets &c &c from their Christmas Tree. We got home by eight o'clock and had tea and got to bed.

Thursday the 5th, Last Lesson

Got to the Castle at one. The day before I expressed a wish to have all the Children's portraits and this morning each of the Princesses came into the room carrying her own portrait which they presented to me from the Queen of which I felt very proud. They all had their lesson and we got home to dinner at three and were back again to the Castle at six. The Prince of Wales and Prince Alfred brought me their portraits and presented them to me in the same way. The Princes had their lesson and we got home by eight o'clock.

Friday the 6th, No lesson

I went by appointment to the Castle at ten to meet McDonald to get a ride on the brake to Prince Albert's Flemish Farm to see His Royal Highness shoot. We got to the ground by eleven and after waiting for some time the Prince with a party of Gentlemen drove up. McDonald told the Prince that he had taken the liberty to bring me as I felt anxious to see the sport. The Prince said "Most certainly" and asked me to come along with him and I had the honour to walking by his side the whole day. The snow was very deep, over the knees at every step. The Prince said to me "I hope you are not in your dancing pumps, Mr Lowe," I said to His Royal Highness that this kind of work would not answer very well for them. He asked me by name very frequently to beat some of the bushes for him and I frequently started some pheasants and hares which His Royal Highness invariably knocked down. He is a first rate shot and very seldom misses if he has a fair chance. I saw him very often make very clever and long shots, as the pheasants passed between the trees. There were three other guns. Colonel Phipps shot beautifully, I saw him make some very clever shots also and almost every time brought down his bird. There was 136 head of game killed but the Prince killed by far the most. After the Prince and his party left, the Keepers amused themselves in killing small birds to empty the guns. McDonald is a good shot, he killed several blackbirds on the wing very neatly. We got back to the Castle by half past three, I went to McDonald's house to met Charlotte where we had dinner. We got home before six and packed our trunks. I then went to supper with Mackay and got home by twelve and went to bed.

Saturday the 7th

After breakfast I went up to Windsor to settle some accounts and to enquire about the trains for London. Took a cab home with me to carry us to the station. We started at half past twelve and were in London before two. Sent Charlotte to Mrs Robson's at Kensington and went myself to Webb's Hotel. I went to the Haymarket Theatre and got back to the hotel by twelve, had a welsh rabbit and a tumbler of rum toddy, and went to bed.

Sunday the 8th

I walked about London the whole day. Went and saw the Thames Tunnel and got to Kensington at five. Remained at Mrs Robson's till nine, I then went home to my hotel, had something to drink then went to bed.

Monday the 9th

Made some calls in London and by an accident I met Mr Micheau. We had something together, I then went to meet Charlotte at Mr Laurier's where we dined. After dinner we went to meet Mr Micheau by appointment at five, had a long chat with him, got to the hotel by eight, paid my bill and had all the trunks put out. Charlotte and Miss Laurier then came, got all the trunks put on the coach, and drove to the railway station, got tickets &c and started at half past nine, and arrived in Edinburgh by ten next morning, much pleased with our visit.

14. Queen Victoria in a carriage accompanied by the Princess Royal (with umbrella), the Prince of Wales and Princess Alice, February 10th 1857.

Photographer: W. Bambridge. Copyright Windsor Castle. Royal Archives. (c) 1991. Her Majesty The Queen.

V. Third Visit to Balmoral to Teach the Royal Children Dancing and Calisthenics in September 1854

Left Inverness on the 14th of September by the Queen Steamer for Aberdeen. Arrived in Aberdeen on the 15th and remained all night. Took the railway to Banchory on the 16th, had dinner then got the coach to Ballater. Had to remain there all night, there not being any conveyance any farther up Deeside that evening. Next morning, Sunday 17th, hired a dog cart to drive me and my luggage to Balmoral. Got to my lodgings by one. In the evening Mr McDonald and Ross the new Piper called. We had some toddy, I took a walk with them towards the Castle, and got home to bed by nine o'clock.

Monday the 18th

Went to the Castle by nine o'clock to announce my arrival to Colonel Phipps. The Colonel sent a Footman to inform Her Majesty that I had come, and in about an hour a Messenger went sent for me to be in the Ball Room at a quarter past one. Went for my fiddle and on the way met Mr Gibbs the Tutor, the Prince of Wales and Prince Alfred, loaded with toys to give away amongst the poor cottagers' children. The Princes ran up to me and shook hands with me very kindly. I got to the Ball Room at the time appointed and in a short time Miss Hildyard brought me the Princess Alice and the Princess Royal who also very kindly shook hands with me. They had a short lesson then went to lunch and I went to dinner. After dinner I had Prince Alfred for a Fiddle lesson and was told that the others were going out and would not dance any today. I then went home, I then went to have a walk with Johnnie in the woods. Before we got far Mr Gibbs and the two Princes rode up to us and, as soon as they recognised us, they hollered out my name and rode up to Johnnie and shook hands with him and seemed quite delighted to see him. When they rode on we had a long walk amongst the woods of Abergeldie, and as we were turning a corner the Queen and Prince Albert drove up. Her Majesty ordered the carriage to stop, and the Prince beckoned on me to come forward. Her Majesty asked me very kindly how I was and how I had left my daughters and all my family which, from the kindly manner in which Her Majesty addressed me, I felt very proud and thought it very condescending. They then drove on, and we went home and had tea. In the evening Willie Blair called and played a few of his Highland Strathspeys and Reels. He left at eight o'clock. I wrote this day's Journal and some letters, then went to bed at eleven.

V. BALMORAL, SEPTEMBER, 1854

Tuesday the 19th

Got to the Castle at quarter past nine to give Prince Alfred his Fiddle and Dancing lesson, His Royal Highness had half an hour at each. John and I then went out and walked about the grounds and through the new Castle till one. I then went to the Ball Room and had the Princess Royal and the Princess Alice for half an hour. They both seemed quite fatigued with a long walk they had had and could not take a proper lesson. I got home by four o'clock, had a long walk, got home and had tea and to bed by ten o'clock.

Wednesday the 20th

Got to the Castle by nine o'clock, gave Prince Alfred his Music and Dancing lesson after which John and I had a walk. I got back to the Ball Room before one and had the Princess Helena for a short lesson. Prince Albert came into the room and saw part of the lesson, Miss Hildyard then brought me the Princess Royal for her lesson principally in Calisthenic Exercises. Then the Princess Alice came and had her lesson. All was over by half past one, I then had dinner and got home by half past three. Had a long walk, came home had tea, fiddled a little, read the newspapers and got to bed by ten.

Thursday the 21st

Got the Castle by nine, gave Prince Alfred his Music and Dancing lesson then walked about till twelve. Got to the Ball Room and had the Princess Helena, then the Prince of Wales and the Princesses Royal and Alice. Got all over by two o'clock, had dinner and got home before four o'clock. Had some fiddling, read the newspapers and to bed by ten o'clock.

Friday the 22nd

Got to the Castle by nine o'clock, gave Prince Alfred his Music and Dancing lesson then went and surveyed all the new Castle with John. When looking at the new Ball Room Prince Albert came up to me and said "This is to be your apartment Mr Lowe." The Prince walked all round the new building with me and told me all the particulars about it. The Queen then came and said "How do you do Mr Lowe." After a little the Queen and the Prince left and John and I had a walk up the river side. I then went to the Ball Room and met the Princess Royal and the Princess Alice who had their lesson in Calisthenics and Dancing, after which I had dinner and was on my way home when a messenger came running up to me and said "Mr Lowe, you are wanted at the Castle." I went back and met the whole of the Royal Children in the Ball Room. They all danced Country Dances and Reels for nearly an hour then left. I then went home, had tea, wrote some letters, and to bed by ten o'clock.

Saturday the 23rd

Nothing particular occurred. Gave my usual lessons and got home by four o'clock, fiddled a while, read a while and got to bed by ten o'clock.

Sunday the 24th

Very bad day, stopped at home, saw the Queen drive past to Church, went and dined at the Castle, came home to tea and got to bed by ten o'clock.

Monday the 25th

Got to the Castle by nine and gave Prince Alfred his Music and Dancing lesson, then the Prince of Wales came and had a Dancing lesson, John dancing with him all the time. Miss Hildyard then brought me the Princess Royal and the Princess Alice. Before their lesson commenced they asked me to let John dance his Highland Fling which he did in style. They all seemed delighted with him. They then had their regular lesson, and left. I went to dinner, and got home by four o'clock, wrote some music for Prince Alfred, and got to bed by ten o'clock.

Tuesday the 26th

Went to the Castle at the usual time, gave all the usual lessons to the Princes and Princesses. Had dinner and got home by four o'clock, read the newspapers and fiddled for a while and got to bed by ten o'clock.

Wednesday the 27th

Got to the Castle by nine o'clock and gave the usual lessons to the Princes and Princesses. Had dinner and got home by four o'clock, read and fiddled for a time and to bed by ten.

Thursday the 28th

Got to the Castle by nine o'clock, gave Prince Alfred his Music and Dancing lesson, then the Prince of Wales came and had a lesson with John dancing as his partner. Then Miss Hildyard brought the Princess Royal and the Princess Alice to their lesson. I got all over by two o'clock, had dinner, then went out to fish with Mr Gibbs. Only caught four trout and got home at seven, had tea and got to bed by ten.

Friday the 29th

Got to the Castle by nine and had the Princes of Wales first. He danced with John for half an hour, then Prince Alfred came and had half an hour

V. BALMORAL, SEPTEMBER–OCTOBER, 1854

at his Violin and half an hour at his Dancing lesson. The Princess Helena was then brought to me to have her lesson. While I was engaged with the lesson, Her Majesty and Prince Albert came into the room and saw the Princess Helena take part of her lesson. Her Majesty only bowed to me on this occasion but the Prince, (who is very sharp) noticed the great fault of the Princess Helena turning in her left foot. His Royal Highness spoke to me about it, the Queen and the Prince then left the room and Miss Hildyard then brought me the Princess Royal and the Princess Alice. They went through all their steps and exercises and all was over by two. I had dinner and got to my lodgings by four, got my fishing rod and went out to fish but only caught six small trout. This day I gave the Prince of Wales some nice trout flies. Got home and to bed by ten.

Saturday the 30th

Gave my lesson in Music and Dancing to Prince Alfred. His Royal Highness, very childlike, told me that he had seen the pretty flies that I had given to the Prince of Wales and I of course had to give him some of the same. I gave all the usual lessons, saw Colonel Phipps and the Colonel gave me a seat in the special Messengers' Carriage to Perth. Got home by four o'clock, and packed my trunks, and got to bed by ten.

Sunday the 1st

Got McDonald to take luggage to the Castle, got it packed on the carriage. Saw some of my friends and started for Perth at eleven o'clock. Had a splendid ride all through Braemar and got to Perth between five and six o'clock. Called on my nephew John and spent the evening.

Monday the 2nd

Took the Railway to Edinburgh and arrived at one o'clock and commenced lessons immediately.

VI. Third Visit to Windsor Castle to Teach the Royal Children in 1854 and 1855

Left Edinburgh with my daughter Charlotte on Thursday the 21st of December 1854 by the North British Railway at eight am for Newcastle, intending to stop for the night to see Mr D'Albert's Ball. But on our arrival received an extraordinary letter from D'Albert stating that I could not be admitted as he would not admit professional persons to see his pupils dance. I of course felt disappointed as he and I had always been on such friendly terms, and cannot account for this piece of caprice. We went to the Turk's Head and had dinner, then walked out to see the town, and spent rather a tiresome evening. Got to the Railway Station between twelve and one, and started for London at half past one, and arrived in London by ten o'clock on Friday morning. Had a cab and drove to Webb's Hotel in Piccadilly, took off our luggage and sent Charlotte by the omnibus to Kensington to see Mrs Robson. Had a jolly good breakfast then went out to walk about. Called on Mr Muller and heard him play over a great many of his new arrangements of Reels and Strathspeys. He went with me to call for Mr Lock, *who* made us go with him to dinner to his country house at Brompton. Had a capital dinner and plenty of whisky toddy, then set to the fiddling of Reels and spent a very pleasant night. Got back to the hotel about twelve and went to bed.

Saturday the 23rd

Had breakfast at ten, went out and called on Moucatell, saw some fine violins then went on to Leicester Square and spent two hours in the large Globe, where I saw a beautiful model of Sebastopol and the position of all the armies in the country, Balaklava, Inkermann &c &c. I then went to the hotel and had some soup, packed my portmanteaux, called for Charlotte at Mr Laurier's in St James Street, drove to the Paddington Station and got the Train for Windsor at four pm. Got to Windsor at five, left our luggage at the station, and went to see about a lodging. Got a very good lodging in Wellington Place, went back for our luggage, bought some tea and sugar &c &c, and went to the lodging. Had tea, then wrote a note to Colonel Phipps announcing our arrival, took it to the Castle, then took a walk through Windsor. Bought a box to hold our stores as there was no press in the lodgings and got home by nine o'clock. Wrote so much of this Journal and got to bed by eleven.

VI. WINDSOR, DECEMBER, 1854

Sunday the 24th

A very wet day, stopped in the house till after dinner then went and called for Mrs Gibbs where I used to lodge. Then went to the Home Park to call for Mrs McDonald where we spent the evening, got home by eleven.

Monday the 25th, Christmas Day

Went to the Castle in the morning, saw Colonel Phipps who told me that there would be no lesson that day. We went and had our Christmas Dinner with Mr McDonald and got home by eleven o'clock and went to bed.

Tuesday the 26th

Went early to the Castle and saw Miss Hildyard and got Orders to be in attendance at one for the younger Princesses. We got to the Castle in good time and went to the Red Drawing Room. Shortly after Miss Illhardt, the German Governess, brought us the Princess Helena and the Princess Louise. They had both a long lesson in Dancing and Calisthenics. We got Orders to be back again at five to meet the elder Princesses. We got there in good time and after remaining in the Red Drawing Rom for some time, Miss Hildyard brought us the Princess Royal and the Princess Alice. They were very glad to see us and shook hands very kindly. They had both a very good lesson for nearly an hour, then left. We also left as the Princes were not to take a lesson that night. We went home to tea and after reading and fiddling for a time got to bed by eleven.

Wednesday the 27th

Got to the Castle at one and gave the two younger Princesses their lesson. Got home to dinner before three, then dressed and back to the Castle at five and had the elder Princesses for nearly an hour. Got home to tea and to bed by eleven.

Thursday the 28th

Everything the same as the day before.

Friday the 29th

Everything the same as the day before excepting that Colonel Seymour's little girl danced with the elder Princesses in the evening.

Saturday the 30th

Got to the Castle at one and had the younger Princesses. Got home to dinner, got back at five and had the Princess Royal and the Princess Alice with the four daughters of Lady Mary Labouchere. We were asked to remain for an hour as they all wished to have a dance together in the evening. At seven o'clock every one of the Royal Children came in with all their young friends, the nurses carrying Prince Arthur and Prince Leopold to let us see them. This was the first time that we had seen Prince Leopold, a fine little fellow and very like the others. They all had a nice dance. First a Country Dance Pop Goes the Weasel, where Charlotte had the honour of leading Prince Arthur through his first dance, then Reels, Quadrille &c. In an hour they all left, there were 19 in the room that night. We got home to tea and to bed at eleven.

Sunday the 31st

Had breakfast at half past nine. McDonald's eldest son called and we set off to see the scenery about Virginia Water, a long walk of eight miles from Windsor, the scenery is very beautiful indeed. After walking all round the lake and visiting every place worth seeing we got to the White Sheafe Inn by three o'clock and had a capital dinner and a long rest. Then started back again for Windsor, a seven miles walk, where we arrived about eight o'clock. Charly stood it out beautifully and did not seem very much fatigued. We got to bed very soon and slept soundly.

Monday the 1st

No lesson at the Castle this day. We went to McDonald's. I got a fishing rod rigged out to try with salmon roe in the Thames but did not get a single bite. We came home to dinner at four then went to the Castle at seven to see the Royal Table laid out for a dinner of thirty. No one could describe the magnificent show of gold and silver ornaments, rich bouquets, golden candelabra, &c. The Christmas Trees of the Queen, the Duchess of Kent, and the Royal Children all lighted up at the end of the room had a magnificent appearance. When the Royal Party went in to dinner Charlotte and I went into the Grand Corridor and spent an hour looking at the exquisite pictures and statuary. We had tickets given to us for a Grand Concert that was to take place in St George's Hall that evening, and went to McDonald's room and waited till the time that the concert was to commence. We got into the Gallery of St George's Hall at nine. There were a good many of the Nobility in the room and the orchestra quite filled with the performers, 150 in number. Miss C. Novello and Mrs Weiss, Mr Sims Reeves and Mr Weiss the principal singers, led by Mr Sainton the violinist, Mr Anderson the conductor. The

15. Queen Victoria's Christmas Tree and table of presents, 1857.

Queen Victoria and Prince Albert popularised the German custom of decorating trees at Christmas which had been introduced into England at the time of George III. At Windsor members of the Royal Family and household had trees and tables of presents which were distributed on Christmas Eve. New Year's Day concert and Twelfth Night theatricals were part of the ceremonies and festivities of the season which Joseph Lowe witnessed on several occasions.

Queen Victoria records in her Journal for the 1st January 1855:

After dinner we had some very fine music in St. George's Hall, really the finest of any of those performances we have had. There was an orchestra of 140 & chorus of 75. Beethoven's Cantata "The Praise of Music" & Mendelssohn's "Walpurgis Night" were given. The latter was quite splendid. The solo singers were Mme Clara Novello, Mrs Weiss, Mr Sims Reeves, & Mr Weiss. He sang remarkably well, & has a fine voice & so has his wife. The whole was conducted by Mr Anderson.

Photographer: Dr Ernest Becker. Copyright Windsor Castle. Royal Archives. (c) 1991. Her Majesty The Queen.

Queen and the Royal Family came into the room at ten and the concert began with a selection from Beethoven. This would have been very dull and monotonous had it not been for a beautiful piece sung by Miss Novello with an obligato violin accompaniment by Sainton. This was truly beautiful. Between the parts the Queen made the circuit of the room and shook hands and bowed to everyone. The Duchess of Kent did the same. The second part was by Mendelssohn all sparkling and lively throughout. The concert ended about twelve, the Queen then bowed and went out. The band immediately struck up God Save the Queen in the grandest style imaginable, Miss Novello and Sims Reeves taking the solo parts. We got home by half past twelve and went to bed.

Tuesday the 2nd

Had a note from Miss Illhardt the German Governess, requesting us to be at the castle at half past eleven for the younger Princesses. Got there in time and gave them a long lesson. We then left and went to call for Mrs Gibbs our old landlady. After sitting with Mrs Gibbs for some time we left and got home for dinner at three. After dinner we dressed and got back to the Castle at five and had the Princess Royal and the *Princess* Alice. The Duchess of Cambridge and the Princess Mary of Cambridge came with them to see the lesson. They then had some waltzing, Charlotte had the honour of waltzing with the Princess Mary and also with both the Royal Princesses. We got home by seven, had tea wrote some letters and got to bed by eleven.

Wednesday the 3rd

Had Mr McDonald's boys in the morning, then went to the Castle for the younger Princesses, gave them a long lesson and went home to dinner. Dressed and went back to the Castle at five, and had the Princess Royal and the Princess Alice. We were told that the Queen was to be in to have a dance. After a while Her Majesty came in in excellent spirits, she conversed with me quite freely and asked me to put her in mind of the Reel steps she had learned. She then placed herself before me and took a regular lesson and had a hearty laugh at every mistake that she made. She told me that it was all very easy when she had me to show her, but the moment that I left she forgot all the Steps. She then asked Charlotte to dance a Reel with her. The Party were The Queen, the Princess Royal, the Princess Alice, and Charlotte. Her Majesty said it made her so very hot that she must sit down to rest. The Princess Royal then danced her Irish Steps but did not dance them very well. The Queen then asked Charlotte to dance them which she did and got great praise from the whole of them. Her Majesty got very funny and began to quiz the Princess Royal about shaking her shoulders. She stood up and shook herself, mimicking the Princess Royal, and told me it was like some of the country girls at Balmoral. After a good deal of conversation they all left in the best of spirits. Her Majesty said that I was to tell Mr Roberts to show us all over the castle. We got home by seven, then went to have tea with Mrs Gibbs and spend the evening. Spent a very pleasant evening and got home and to bed by twelve o'clock.

Thursday the 4th

Gave McDonald's boys their lesson in the morning and got to the Castle at one. Had only the Princess Helena, the Princess Louise being ill. Gave the lesson and got home to dinner before three. Dressed and back to the Castle at five and had the Princess Royal and the Princess Alice for their last lesson as they were going in the morning with the Queen to Osborne. They went through all the usual lesson, waltzed a good deal with Charlotte then shook hands with us both and bade us goodbye hoping to meet with me again at Balmoral in summer. We then left and got home to tea by seven and to bed by eleven.

Friday the 5th

Gave McDonald's boys their lesson in the morning, and got to the Castle at one. Had only the Princess Helena, Louise being still unwell. The Princess Helena brought some very pretty little presents for my youngest boy John. After the lesson she and the Governess bade us good bye. We then went home to dinner, then went to spend the evening at McDonald's where we met with a Mr Menzies and Mr Wilson, two genuine Scotsmen both fond of fiddling. Mr Menzies sent *for* his bass and we spent a jolly night and got home to bed by one.

Saturday the 6th

Went to the Castle in the morning to see Colonel Phipps *but* was rather too late as the Colonel was placed in a carriage going out to shoot. I told him that it was of no consequence and begged that he would not come out for me, as a settlement could be made by writing. Had a chat with McDonald and then went home to pack my trunk and left Windsor by the 12.25 train for London. Arrived in London in an hour, got a cab and drove to Webb's Hotel in Piccadilly, put Charlotte in an omnibus for Kensington where she was going to spend a day with Mrs Robson. I then had some dinner and in the evening I went to Astley's to see The Battle of Alma and was very much pleased with the spectacle. Got to the hotel by twelve, had a rabbit then went to bed.

Sunday the 7th

After breakfast I called for Mr Muller, did not find him at home. Then went to call for Mr Blagrove. He was in Manchester, saw Mrs Blagrove and had a long chat with her. I then went to the end of Oxford Street and through the parks across the Serpentine, into Kensington Gardens and to Kensington to meet Charlotte and to dine with Mrs Robson. Spent a very pleasant evening, and got to the hotel before ten, read the newspapers and went to bed.

Monday the 8th

After breakfast called for Mr Lock, he took me to the Vernon Gallery of Pictures then to the National Gallery. We then called for Mr Muller and sat a long time with him and had plenty of music and wine. I then walked a good way with Mr Lock on his way home and got back to the hotel by five, had some dinner then got my luggage ready. Charlotte called at seven, I got a cab and drove to the King's Cross Station. We got the night train for Edinburgh at nine and arrived at home by half past nine next morning after spending a very pleasant visit.

16. Joseph Lowe's Receipt for the payment for two visits in 1854.
Edinburgh, February 3rd 1855

£80 Recieved from Colonel Phipps the sum of Eighty pounds sterling for attendance at Balmoral and at Windsor Castle to teach the Royal children Dancing and Calisthenic Exercises in 1854, Joseph Lowe

Copyright Windsor Castle. Royal Archives. Archive number pp 2/8/5143 (c) 1991. Her Majesty The Queen.

VII. Mr Lowe's Fourth Visit to Balmoral to Teach Dancing and Calisthenic Exercises in September 1855

Left Inverness on the 16th of September by the Evening Mail at twelve o'clock. Got to Huntly by half past seven am, got the Railway to Aberdeen and arrived there by ten. Went to a Coffee Room with Mr Baillie *the* younger of Dochfour and had breakfast. Then went and called for Mrs R. Alexander. Got the Railway to Banchory at half past twelve, and arrived there at two. Had to wait in Banchory till six for the starting of the Dee Side Coach, arrived at Aboyne at eight, had tea then went to bed.

Tuesday the 18th

Had breakfast at Aboyne at nine then walked about till eleven, then got the coach to Crathie and arrived there at two, got a cart to take my luggage to my lodgings at Easter Balmoral where I found everything ready for me. I then wrote a note to Colonel Phipps announcing my arrival and stating that I would call upon him for Orders in the morning. I then went and had a long walk and called for Willie Blair at Abergeldie, came home and had tea, read for some time then went to bed.

Wednesday the 19th

Had breakfast at half past eight and got to the Castle by ten. Sent up my card to Colonel Phipps and after waiting for a long time I was sent for by Miss Hildyard the Governess to her own room. There was to be no lesson this day but was asked to be at the Castle by half past eight on the following morning to give a lesson in Calisthenics to the Princess Royal and Princess Alice. I then had dinner at the Castle then went to see all the improvements on the river side and in the grounds about the Castle. Met Lady Augusta Bruce on horseback. Her ladyship was at a considerable distance from me on an upper road but she beckoned to me and I went up to her and had a long chat with Her Ladyship. I got home by seven and had tea, I then asked in a dancing master who was living in the same lodgings and had some fiddling with him then went to bed at ten.

Thursday the 20th

Got to the Castle by half past eight and had the Princess Royal and the Princess Alice. They received me very kindly and took a short lesson in Calisthenics. Was ordered back at one to give the Princess Helena and the Princess Louise a Dancing lesson but when I got there I was told that the Queen had them at lunch and that they could not have a lesson at that time. I then went to dinner at two. While I was enjoying my wine after dinner one of the Footmen came and told me that the younger Princesses were in the Dancing Room waiting for me. I went and gave them a fair lesson but not nearly so long as I could have wished *as* they were engaged to go out and could not remain with me. I then came home and wrote a letter to Lizzey to Brussels and so far of this Journal. Took my letter to the Crathie Post Office then came home, read the newspapers and got to bed by ten.

Friday the 21st

Went to the Castle at one and gave the Princess Helena and the Princess Louise a lesson then went to dinner. Was sent for at half past three to give the Princess Royal and the Princess Alice their lesson. They only remained for half an hour and left. On my way home I met Mr Gibbs, the Prince of Wales and Prince Alfred. I asked if they were not to have any Dancing lesson this season and was told that they danced well enough and that they would only join when there was a general Dance. Got home by seven, had tea, read and wrote and to bed before ten.

Saturday the 22nd

Went to the Castle at half past eight and gave the Princess Royal and the *other* Princesses a lesson. Went and took a long walk, and read the Inverness Courier. While sitting on one of the seats in the private grounds reading, a young man with very red hair came close to me and was breaking away at some of the rocks about. I spoke to him and said that I fancied he would find all the rocks in this quarter much of the same kind. He said that he found that to be the case and after come common place talk he went away, but to my great surprise when I got near the Castle I saw this same red haired young man leaning over the Queen's Carriage and carrying on a lively conversation with Her Majesty. It was the Duke of Argyle whom I took for some poor geological student. When I got to the Castle, first one and then another of the Footmen told me that they had been looking for me everywhere for more than an hour as Miss Byng, one of the Maids of Honour, wished to see me. I went immediately to the Dancing Room, met Mr Whiting, one of the Pages, who also told me that Miss Byng had been asking about me. Mr Whiting went and brought Miss Byng to the Dancing Room where I gave her a short lesson and appointed to meet her again on Monday at eleven. I then went to dinner at two and had to be in the Dancing Room by three to meet the younger Princesses. Just as the lesson began, Mr Gibbs came and asked me if I would go out with him and Prince Alfred to fish. He asked Miss Illhardt the Governess to allow me to give a short lesson and told me that a horse would be waiting for me. I gave the

17. The Prince of Wales, Prince Albert and others, 1857

From left: Colonel Phipps, Mr Gibbs, the Prince of Wales, Prince Albert, Baron Stockmar, Dr Becker, and Ernst Stockmar (son of Baron Stockmar). (see members of the Royal Household, Appendix)

The education and care of the Royal Children involved a group of nurses, governesses, tutors and advisors. The principles set down by Albert and Victoria as early as 1840 involved opportunities for the children to enjoy their parents' company, proper religious instruction, the use of European languages, fresh air and exercise, healthy diet and immunization (a new discovery). Albert developed the model kitchen and carpentry workshop at Osborne for their play; rudeness to servants was not permitted; opportunities for music, theatricals and outdoor pursuits were provided. Though much was idealistic the education had the devoted energies of Lady Lyttelton, Miss Hildyard, Mr Gibbs, Joseph Lowe and others. Only with the Prince of Wales was the early education a failure: the fervent hope of the Queen that the Prince of Wales would "resemble his angelic dearest father in every respect both in body and mind" was a disastrous load to place on the young Prince.

Photographer: Caldesi. Copyright Windsor Castle. Royal Archives. (c) 1991. Her Majesty The Queen.

Princesses nearly an hour and then went away to meet Mr Gibbs and Prince Alfred. When I came out of the Court the first thing I saw was a fine spirited horse dashing over the lawn with one of the Grooms upon him. He threw the groom over a paling and ran away to the Stable. This was the horse ordered for me. When he was brought back to me I confess that I felt a little afraid to mount him, but I did mount and got on very well till I came near my own lodgings where a quantity of water had been spilt across the dry road. The horse pricked up his ears and wheeled right round about and would not pass the black mark for some time. I urged him very severely and at last he took a spring over it and very nearly threw me and would have run off had I not held him very hard. I very soon overtook Mr Gibbs and Prince Alfred and we went to a burn near Abergeldie. I put up the Prince's rod and set him agoing but he was sticking his hooks in the trees and bushes every minute. At last they asked me to try and in a very short time I got a nice trout. The Prince tried again and so did Mr Gibbs but they could not manage amongst so many bushes and I got the rod again and in less than an hour I landed 12 very fine yellow trout and lost as many more by allowing Prince Alfred to take the line in his hand to pull them out after they were hooked. One of the Gillies held the horses till we finished, then we all rode home together, the young Prince of course very much delighted with his basket of fish. He took them to the Queen directly and was complimented on his good sport. I came home and wrote this day's Journal, had tea, read the newspaper, and went to bed by ten.

Sunday the 23rd

Went to the Church at Crathie, the Queen, the Prince, the Prince of Prussia, the Duke of Argyle, Lord Granville and several others of the Nobility present. Went to the Castle to dinner then had a long walk with Mr McDonald. In returning we met the Queen, the Prince and all the Royal Family. The Queen asked me "How do you do Mr Lowe" and asked how the Princesses were getting on, then passed on. The Prince said to me, as I stood to the side of the road till they passed, "Mr Lowe that wet grass cannot be good for you. It will bring you rheumatism." I called with McDonald on one of his friends, and came home, and to bed by ten.

Monday the 24th

Got to the Castle by half past eight and gave the Princess Royal and the Princess Alice their lesson then took a walk till eleven. When I got to the Castle and had Miss Byng for an hour, I then waited in the room till one when I had the Princess Helena and the Princess Louise. Got over before two then went to dinner and got home by four. Went back to the Castle

VII. BALMORAL, SEPTEMBER, 1855

at nine to see Basker the Conjuror perform. There was a large party with the Queen in the Iron Ball Room, the Queen, the Prince and all the Royal Family, the Prince of Prussia, the Duchess of Kent, the Duke of Argyle, Lady Augusta Bruce, Lord and Lady Canning, Lord Granville and many others, in all from 40 to 50 in the Queen's Party, all the Servants of the Household and also the Servants from the Duchess of Kent's, the Tenantry on the estate and everyone about the place. They were all seemingly very much pleased with the different tricks, the Queen laughing and enjoying it as much as any of them and drawing a card &c &c from the conjuror the same as anyone else. I got home by twelve o'clock and went to bed.

Tuesday the 25th

Got to the Castle at half past eight and gave the Princess Royal and the Princess Alice a lesson. Went out to walk and got back to meet Miss Byng at eleven. She was called by the Queen to go with Her Majesty to Lochnagar and had no lesson. I stopped in the room till one and then had the Princess Helena and the Princess Louise and gave them their lesson, then went to dinner. Got home by four o'clock, wrote and read all the evening, and got to bed at ten.

Wednesday the 26th

Got to the Castle at half past eight and gave a lesson to the elder Princesses. Met Miss Byng at eleven and gave her a lesson and had the younger Princesses at one for their lesson. Then went to dinner and got home by four o'clock. Went to the river and caught a few trout then home to tea, and to bed by ten.

Thursday the 27th

Got to the Castle at half past eight and gave the elder Princesses their lesson and, at eleven, I had them again with Lady Augusta Bruce, the Honourable Miss Seymour and Miss Byng. They danced nothing but Reels for nearly an hour, all but Lady Augusta Bruce who remained with me to go over all her Steps. The younger Princesses then came and had their regular lesson and left before two. Then I went to dinner and got home by four and went to the river and caught some small trout. Came home, had tea and to bed by ten.

Friday the 28th

Got to the Castle at half past eight and give the elder Princesses their usual lesson and went out to walk. Got back to the Dancing Room at eleven and had Miss Byng then remained in the room till one when I had the younger

Princesses for their lesson. This day Miss Hildyard got me permission to dedicate The Balmoral Castle Quadrille to Her Majesty. On this evening the Annual Ball for the Tenantry and Servants about the place was held. I was invited and got to the Ball Room at half past nine. The Queen was there, also the Prince, the Prince of Prussia, all the Royal Children, the Duchess of Kent, the Duchess of Wellington, the Duke of Argyle and a number of other distinguished persons were in the room. There was nothing but Reels one after another. The Royal Children danced amongst the peasantry with great spirit and got great praise. The Jig and the Sword Dance was done three or four times by different persons. The Queen and all of them looked very happy and very much pleased. The Royal Children were decidedly the best dancers in the room. Lady Augusta Bruce insisted on me to dance with her but my breathing was so bad that I excused myself. The Royal Party left about twelve and I got home by one, and went to bed, the country people kept it up till five in the morning.

Saturday the 29th

Did not go to the Castle till eleven when I had Miss Byng for a short lesson. I then had the Princess Louise for a short lesson and had nothing more to do this day. The German Governess told me how much the Queen was pleased with the Children's dancing at the Ball. I had dinner then went for a long walk up the other side of the river. I met Miss Hildyard and the Princess Alice in a pony phaeton. They stopped and Miss Hildyard told me again how much the Queen was pleased with the Children's dancing at the Ball. We had a long chat then passed on. In returning home the Prince of Wales, the Prince Alfred and Mr Gibbs rode up to me. They stopped and walked their ponies a long way beside me and we had a deal of conversation. They then said they must ride on to be in time for dinner and bade me goodbye. I got home by half past seven, read for a while and got to bed by ten.

Sunday the 30th

Breakfasted at eight, wrote to Edinburgh and to Lizzey, then went to the Church at Crathie. The Queen, the Prince and the Prince of Prussia came to the Church. Went to the Castle and had dinner, came home and finished my letters, and took them to the Post Office at Crathie. Met Lady Augusta Bruce, Miss Seymour, Miss Byng, Sir George Couper, and other two Gentlemen walking. Lady Augusta was bantering me for not dancing with her and said she would not take any excuse from me the next time she met me in Ball Room. They all stood with me for some time. I then came home, read a while and got to bed by ten.

18. Royal Family Group, 1855

The Royal Family at Balmoral on 29th December 1855 the day of the engagement of the Princess Royal and Prince Frederick William of Prussia. From left: Prince Alfred, Prince Frederick William, Princess Alice, the Prince of Wales, Queen Victoria, Prince Albert, the Princess Royal.

The month of September includes a number of Journal references to the visit of the Prince of Prussia which culminated in his engagement to the 14 year old Princess Royal. This alliance which was unpopular in Britain was hoped by Albert and Victoria to bring the two countries closer, and some liberal influence to Germany. But the early death of Fritz (briefly Frederick III) prevented this being realised. The son of the Princess Royal and the Prince of Prussia, Victoria's first grandchild, became the Kaiser of World War I.

Photographer: George Washington Wilson.

Monday the 1st

Got to the Castle at half past eight. Miss Hildyard told me that the elder Princesses would not take a lesson till three as there was an early breakfast as the Prince of Prussia was leaving that morning. I then took a long walk. All the great people passed me. First there was a kind of omnibus with all the Prince's Servants and luggage, then came the Queen's own carriage with the Queen, Prince Albert and the Prince of Prussia, then another carriage with four horses with all the Prince of Prussia's attendants in it. I got back to the Castle by eleven and gave Miss Byng her lesson and waited in the room till one when I had the younger Princesses for their lesson. Then went to dinner, and back again to the Dancing Room at three to meet the elder Princesses but only had the Princess Alice who had a good lesson. I got home by four o'clock, I went to the river and caught eight trout, came home, had tea, read and wrote for a time, and got to bed by ten.

Tuesday the 2nd

Got to the Castle at half past eight and gave the Princess Alice her lesson. Then Miss Byng came and danced with her for half an hour. They then left and I went out to walk till one when I returned and had Miss Seymour and Miss Byng again. Then the younger Princesses had their lesson. They then danced a Reel together and left at two. I then went to dinner and got home before four, went to the river and caught seven trout, one with the pair tail, a good-sized trout about half a pound. Came home and had tea. Willie Blair called and we had some fiddling together. He left and I got to bed by ten.

Wednesday the 3rd Last Lesson

Got to the Castle at half past eight and gave the Princess Royal and the Princess Alice their lesson and went out to walk. Came back at eleven and gave Miss Byng a lesson, then had the younger Princesses for their lesson at one. Called for Colonel Phipps and told him that I had finished for the season. Got leave from the Colonel to have a seat in the Messengers' Carriage to Perth on the following morning. I got home by four o'clock, had some fiddling in the evening with Willie Blair and got to bed by eleven.

Thursday the 4th

Got up at seven and packed my luggage, paid my lodgings &c, got Sandy McDonald to take my portmanteaux &c to the Castle. Got all packed on the Messengers' Carriage. Went to the Castle and saw some of my friends to bid them good bye, and started with the Messenger at eleven. Had a very splendid ride through Braemar and got to Perth by six o'clock. Found a train just going to start for Edinburgh, got my ticket and arrived in Edinburgh by nine o'clock and found all well.

19. The Princess Royal and Prince Frederick William of Prussia, 1859.

The wedding of the Princess Royal and Prince Frederick William of Prussia took place in January 1859. The Princess Royal's married home in Berlin provided a sanctuary for sisters Helena and Louise after Albert's death when Victoria's mourning allowed no dancing, and no one to be cheerful in the Queen's presence. The voluminous correspondance between the Queen and her daughter reveals a depth of learning, political concerns, and common sense in the Princess Royal.

Photographer: W. Bambridge. Copyright Windsor Castle. Royal Archives. (c) 1991. Her Majesty The Queen.

VIII. Mr and Miss Lowe's Fourth Visit to Windsor to Teach the Royal Family Dancing and Exercises in 1855 and 1856.

Left Edinburgh by the North British Railway at nine fifteen pm, on Thursday December the 20th 1855 and arrived at King's Cross Station in London about eleven next morning, after suffering severely from the excessive cold, the frost during the night being so intense that our breaths on the carriage windows turned into ice immediately. Fortunately we, at the different stations, got hot water pans for our feet which kept them pretty comfortable.

Friday the 21st

After arriving at King's Cross I got a cab and got all our luggage stowed upon it and drove directly to the Paddington Station and got a train just starting for Windsor. We had no time for breakfast. Arrived at Windsor at twelve where we met John McDonald waiting for us to take us to the lodging he had engaged for us. We then had some mutton chops cooked for us and made a good breakfast. We then went out and bought some tea, sugar, candles &c &c and came home and I wrote to Colonel Phipps announcing our arrival, stating that I should call upon him in the morning for Orders. We had tea at five o'clock, read for a while, and went to bed by eight o'clock.

Saturday the 22nd

Breakfasted at nine then went to see Colonel Phipps. The colonel told me that he had announced my arrival to Her Majesty and that I had better go and see Miss Hildyard. I went and sent up my card to Miss Hildyard, she being ill and in bed and I had to wait for a long time till Miss Illhardt the German Governess came in. I then sent up my card to her and told the Footman to say that I was waiting for Orders and after an hour I was asked to Miss Illhardt's room and arrived and arranged to be at the Castle at five o'clock to give the first lesson. While I was waiting the Prince of Wales called from the bottom of a flight of stairs "Ah Mr Lowe how do you do. When did you come to Windsor. How have you been &c &c." And after some remarks on the cold day and fine skating weather he went away. The Princess Alice came into Miss Illhardt's room while I was there. Her Royal Highness came up to me very frankly and shook me by the hand and asked very kindly how I had been since we parted at Balmoral, if I had brought Miss Lowe with me &c &c. Charlotte and I got to the Castle and into the Red Drawing Room by five. Miss Illhardt brought us the Princess Alice, Princess Helena and Princess Louise and also Prince Arthur. Charlotte

VIII. WINDSOR, DECEMBER, 1855

taught the little Prince his Positions while I went over all the Steps with the Princesses. While the Princess Helena was at her lesson Madame Rollande brought in the Princess Royal who asked very kindly for us and shook hands with Charlotte. Miss Byng then came in and after a time the Princess Royal, the Princess Alice, Miss Byng and Charlotte danced a Reel, then the Reel of Tulloch. I then took Prince Arthur to see his Positions and while engaged with him the Queen came in and bowed most graciously to both of us. Her Majesty laughed most heartily at the attempts of the little Prince to change his feet. Her Majesty then wished to dance a Reel which she did with the three elder Princesses. Her Majesty then stood up before me and asked me to put her in mind of some of the Steps that she had forgotten, and took a capital lesson, then left the room. I then gave the Princess Louise a short lesson and made arrangements to be at the Castle at one on Monday. They then all left and we got home before seven and had tea, read and wrote for some time and got to bed by ten.

Sunday the 23rd

A very wet day, stopped in the house all the forenoon, had dinner at one, then went and called for Mrs Gibbs then went and called at the Shaw Farm for Mr Wilson and had some wine. From that we went and called for Mrs McDonald in the Home Park where we had tea and got home by nine o'clock and went to bed.

20. "Balmoral Castle Quadrille"

In December 1855 this publication was completed, and copies given to the Royal Family and music sellers.

The Quadrille is given in full in the Appendix.

Monday the 24th

We got to the Castle before one, and met the younger Princesses in the Red Drawing Room. Gave them and little Prince Arthur a good lesson. I gave copies of The Balmoral Quadrille to the Queen and to the Princess Royal, Alice, to the Governesses, to Colonel Phipps, to Sir James Clark, to Mr Seabrook &c, we got home to dinner by two o'clock, there not being another lesson at the Castle this day. Charlotte went to London to spend Christmas Day and I went and gave copies of The Balmoral Castle Quadrille to the different music sellers and came home. Ross the Queen's Piper called upon me and we had some toddy. I then went to spend the evening at the Shaw Farm with Mr Wilson and met Mr Menzies. We had a regular night's fiddling and a splendid supper and I got home by one o'clock in the morning and went to bed.

Tuesday the 25th

It was my intention to go to London this day, there not being any lesson at the Castle, it being Christmas Day, but the morning being so wet and such a dull foggy day I stayed at home and read all the forenoon, then went and had a chop at the Star Hotel. Took a long walk by Eton and came home, read for some time, got sleepy and went to bed by nine o'clock.

Wednesday the 26th

Charlotte arrived from London at eleven. We got to the Castle at one and had the Princess Helena, Louise and Prince Arthur. They had a long lesson, and we got home by half past two and had dinner. We then dressed and got back to the Castle at four to meet the elder Princesses. The Princess Royal and Alice came and had a good lesson. They both thanked me for the Quadrilles. Miss Illhardt delivered the thanks of the Queen for the copy I gave to her. Before the Princess Alice finished her lesson the Queen came in and asked me to give her a lesson, often repeating, when she went wrong that I must think her very stupid. I told Her Majesty that she had had very little practice and that in these Steps it required a deal of repetition before the practice became a habit, and that I thought Her Majesty did them very well indeed considering the little time she had been learning. The Prince of Wales and Prince Alfred then came and went over some of their Steps, then the Queen and the Princes danced a Reel. The Queen then asked Charlotte to dance the Reel of Tulloch with her. When they met in the middle she took hold of Charlotte's hand behind backs and had a nice swing round without the smallest ceremony. The Prince of Wales had a good

21. Musician: William Ross, the Queen's Piper, 1855

The Queen's pipers, first Mackay and later Ross are frequently met in the Journal, as companions of Joseph Lowe. They were engaged to play at meals (a habit Victoria observed on her first visit to Scotland in 1842) and at Balls and official functions.

The Queen writes in *Our Life in the Highlands*: "Mackay my piper from the year 1843, considered almost the first in Scotland, who was recommended by the Marquis of Breadalbane; he unfortunately went out of his mind in the year 1854, and died in 1855." (page 42 fn)

Willie Blair who was a frequent performer in the band for the Royal Balls at Balmoral was born at Abergeldie. He is describe as "tall, stout and plain of speech and manner. He was apparently much addicted to snuff and often set those near to him sneezing when in the thick of a tune he would snort and puff" (Emmerson 1971 page 102). His sons James and John were both fiddlers, as Willie's father had been before him.

Queen Victoria refers to the death of Willie Blair in 1884, aged 90, commenting that he had played the fiddle at all their Balls at Balmoral since they had first gone there in 1848.

Photographer: J.J.E.Mayall. Copyright Windsor Castle. Royal Archives.
(c) 1991. Her Majesty The Queen.

tumble down on the floor which set them all a laughing very heartily. Her Majesty and the whole of them were very free and very affable, not the least stiffness or ceremony, all seemingly very happy and unreserved. After an hour's good practice, they all left, the Queen bowing most graciously to us both as she retired. We got home by six and had tea, practised the piano and fiddle, read for a time, and to bed by ten o'clock.

Thursday the 27th

No lesson at the Castle till five o'clock. We went in the forenoon to the Round Tower and called for Mrs Jack *and* saw her daughter. We then went and called for Mrs McDonald, came home to dinner at two, dressed for the Castle and got there by five. We first had the Princesses Helena and Louise and Prince Arthur, they all had a good lesson then Miss Hildyard brought the Princess Alice who took a nice lesson. Miss Byng then came and had her lesson after which the Princess Alice, Miss Byng and Charlotte danced a Reel of Three, then the Reel of Tulloch. The Princess Alice got through all La Grace very well indeed and seemed to like the lesson. The Governesses expressed themselves quite delighted with the lesson. They all left at seven o'clock quite pleased and we came home and had tea, wrote, read, and played for some time and went to bed at ten.

Friday the 28th

No lesson at the Castle till five. Gave the McDonald boys their lesson in the morning went to the Castle at five. Gave the younger Princesses and Prince Arthur their usual lesson. Nothing particular occurred and we got home before seven.

Saturday the 29th

No lesson at the Castle till five. I went in the morning to fish in the Thames but only caught one roach, got home to dinner at three then dressed for the Castle, got there by five. We first had the Princess Royal and the Princess Alice for their lesson then the younger Princesses. Miss Byng then came and they all danced together for nearly an hour, then left. We got home by half past seven. The cab was at the door waiting for us to take us to Mr Menzies' at Park Side in Windsor Forest near Virginia Water, five miles from Windsor. We arrived there about half past eight, had tea, then commenced fiddling and spent a happy evening, we remained all night.

VIII. WINDSOR, DECEMBER, 1855–JANUARY, 1856

Sunday the 30th

After breakfast we all walked to the Chapel in Windsor Forest and had a good sermon. Met Mr Wilson at the Church, he came to dinner with us at Park Side but had to leave immediately after. Mr Menzies, Charlotte and I had a long walk through the forest to Virginia Water, the afternoon very fine and the scenery very beautiful. We got back to Park Side in the darkening, had tea and remained all night.

Monday the 31st

Our cab came to Park Side by nine o'clock and after breakfast we started for Windsor and arrived there shortly after ten. I gave McDonald's boys a lesson and we got to the Castle at twelve to give the Princess Alice a lesson in the Spanish Guaracha. She got four Steps and was quite pleased with it. We got home to dinner before two. I wrote some letters, had dinner and back to the Castle again by five. The younger Princesses and Prince Arthur had a long lesson. We got home again by seven had tea &c.

Tuesday the 1st

No lesson at the Castle this day. I made arrangements with McDonald to go into Windsor Forest to see Prince Albert and a party shooting. McDonald called for me at my lodgings with their carriage and drove me to the Shooting Grounds about five miles from Windsor. We got to the appointed place by half past ten where we met about 40 Keepers with a set of beagle retrievers and a number of Foresters making a gathering of about 60 people. In a short time Prince Albert, Prince Ernest of Leiningen, Prince Edward of Saxe Weimar, the Duke of Cambridge, the Duke of Newcastle and several other Noblemen rode up. Prince Albert whenever he saw me said "How do you do Mr Lowe. I am glad to see you." The Keepers then loaded the guns and handed them to the different shooters. The whole party then walked for a short distance to the first cover that was to be scoured. We were then all formed in a long line, the different guns at equal distances along the line. The word "Forward" was given, then the shouting and thrashing the bushes with sticks commenced, and in a few minutes the rabbits were started in hundreds and rolling over in all directions. The firing was constant, it could not have been more so at Alma. The poor pheasants were tumbling down in dozens, many splendid shots were made and many shameful misses. Prince Albert was by the far the quickest and most deadly shot in the Party. He very seldom missed when there was any chance of hitting. Each of the Shooters had two double guns and a Keeper to load, but so very fast did the rabbits and pheasants get up that the Keepers could not load fast enough to keep the Shooters going. Prince Albert had three guns and two Loaders and whenever one gun was discharged another loaded and ready was put into his hand. They made great slaughter in this cover then went to another and another and repeated the same thing. At one time when Colonel Seymour was questioning me as to who I was and who I came with, Prince Albert called to me to come and examine some beautiful trees and said *that* we have nothing like that in Scotland. I know that this was done to show Colonel Seymour that I was personally known to His Royal Highness. After not more than two hours' shooting the party left. The game was then counted. There were in all 202 pheasants, 240 rabbits, 8 hares, 4 roe deer, and 3 woodcocks, tremendous slaughter in two hours. The line in going through the different covers was kept by Colonel Seymour in regular military order and the word of command given such as "Advance Right Wing" or "Advance Left Wing," "Steady Centre Position" or "Advance Centre Position" &c &c. No one was allowed to keep behind or to advance before the line. This was necessary to prevent accidents as very often the birds flew over our heads and the Shooters had to turn quickly round to shoot them. There was a luncheon brought to the place where the game was counted for all the Keepers, plenty of beef, bread and good ale which soon disappeared. The guns were all put into the cases and then into McDonald's carriage and we mounted and drove home. I went to McDonald's to dinner to meet Charlotte. We spent the evening there and got home by twelve o'clock and to bed.

Wednesday the 2nd

Gave McDonald's boys a lesson in the morning and got to the Castle at one and gave the younger Princesses and Prince Arthur their lesson and got home to dinner between two and three. Got back to the Castle again at half past six, gave the Princess Alice and Miss Byng a lesson and got home before eight.

Thursday the 3rd

Had McDonald's boys after breakfast and got to the Castle at one. We had the younger Princesses and Prince Arthur for an hour and got home to dinner at two. Back to the Castle again at six, we had the Princess Royal, Princess Royal, Princess Alice, and Miss Byng for an hour and as we were leaving we met the Queen in the corridor. Her Majesty asked me to return to the Drawing Room as she wished to have a lesson. She then immediately *we were leaving we met the Queen in the Corridor Her Majesty asked me as to return to the Drawing Room as she wished to have a lesson, She then immediately stood in before me and went through all her Steps very well indeed, She told me that she practised every day in her own Room and that she now knew them all perfectly and would never forget them any more*

22. The Journal of Joseph Lowe, 3rd January 1856

Queen Victoria especially as a young woman loved to dance, and often expressed herself pleased with the children's accomplishments from Mr Lowe's lessons. She herself frequently had lessons from him and here acknowledges the practise "in her own room," which sets her in a long tradition of dancing monarchs.

---

stood in before me and went through all her Steps very well indeed. She told me that she practised every day in her own room and that she now knew them all perfectly and would never forget them any more. Her Majesty, the Princess Alice and Charlotte then danced a Threesome Reel with great spirit. The Princess Alice then danced all her Steps to the Queen and got great praise. They then left and we got home to tea by eight o'clock.

Friday the 4th

Had McDonald's boys after breakfast and got to the Castle at twelve to give the Princess Alice a good working at her Spanish Dance. Remained for an hour with her. We then called for Mrs Jack but did not see her, and came home to dinner, dressed and got back to the Castle at five. We gave the younger Princesses and Prince Arthur a good lesson and got home by seven and had tea.

Saturday the 5th, Last Lesson

Had McDonald's boys after breakfast and got to the Castle by one. Had the younger Princesses for an hour and got home to dinner before three. Dressed and got back to the Castle at half past four. We first had the Princess Alice for her Spanish Dance for half an hour, she then left to dress in her Spanish Dress to show off before the Queen and we had the little ones again for some time. Then the Nursemaid brought us in the baby to show him to us, Prince Leopold, he is a very pretty, chubby child with a great look of George the Third. All the little ones had a great deal of fun dancing up and down the room with Charlotte, round and round about, in below each other's arms &c &c, asking me to play Pop Goes The Weasel, The Pigs March &c &c. Little Leopold and Prince Arthur had several trials of my fiddle and after a deal of romping the Princess Alice came in dressed in her Spanish Dress and very soon after the Queen and the Princess Royal and some other Ladies came in. The Princess Alice then began her Spanish Dance but was stopped in the middle of it as Prince Albert came into the room. We began it again and she went through it all very much better than I expected. The Queen, the Prince and all of them gave her great praise. The Queen told me that she was very much pleased indeed and that she thought it an excellent exercise for improving the figure and teaching graceful motion. The Princess Helena then danced The Lass of Gourie, not very well but they all seemed quite pleased with it. Prince Albert laughed very heartily and quizzed her about her turned-in toes. We then had sets of Steps, Reels &c. The Queen then asked Charlotte to show her how to beat the castanets and held out her hand for Charlotte to fix them on which put her in a great flutter. After a time spent with this, the Queen wished Charlotte to dance a Reel with her. The party were the Queen, the Princess Alice, the Princess Helena and Charlotte. After this the Queen left bowing goodbye to both of us. The children, the Governesses and Charlotte then danced Pop Goes the Weasel, Charlotte leading little Prince Leopold through the Figure. They then gave Charlotte a number of little presents from their Christmas Tree. They then all shook hands with us and bade us goodbye. Little Prince Arthur kissed Charlotte's hand two or three times in parting. We came and had a party of Scotch friends in the evening. Mr Menzies sent his violincello and we had lots of Scotch music. Had a nice supper and plenty of toddy and kept it up till twelve o'clock, after which they all left quite delighted and we got to bed by one.

VIII. WINDSOR, JANUARY, 1856

Sunday the 6th

Called on Mr Wilson in the forenoon, had some wine &c and bade them goodbye. We then went and had dinner at McDonald's and spent the evening and got home by eleven o'clock.

Monday the 7th

Packed our trunks in the morning, went out and settled some accounts, and started for London at twelve o'clock. Charlotte went to Kensington and after seeing her safe in Mrs Robson's, I drove on to Webb's Hotel in Piccadilly. We spent a week in London and arrived in Edinburgh safe and sound on Saturday morning after a very pleasant visit.

IX. Fifth Visit to Balmoral to Teach the Royal Children 1856

Being not able to go myself this season Miss Lowe and my son Robert went and were very kindly received. Her Journal lost.

X. Fifth Visit to Teach the Royal Children at Windsor Castle in 1856

Started from Edinburgh with Charlotte and Isabella on the 20th of December by the train to Berwick at eight am. Got the express train at Berwick at eleven am and arrived in London at half past nine pm. Got a cab and drove to Webb's Hotel, had tea and got to bed by eleven.

Sunday the 21st

Breakfasted at nine, had Miss Laurier to breakfast. Walked about London till twelve, went and heard a sermon in Westminster Abbey, then went and dined at Mr Laurier's at two. Left at five and drove to the Windsor Station at Waterloo. Got a train to Windsor at half past six and arrived at eight and found our lodgings quite ready for us, had tea and got to bed by ten.

Monday the 22nd

Had breakfast at nine, wrote a letter to Miss Hildyard and one to Colonel Phipps announcing our arrival. In a short time we had a note from Miss Hildyard asking us to be at the Castle at six to give the first lesson. We went out and bought some provisions, hired a piano and came home to dinner. Got to the Castle at six and Miss Hildyard brought us the Princess Royal and the Princess Alice, they took a very short lesson. Then we went to visit Mrs McDonald and did not get home till twelve o'clock, then to bed.

Tuesday the 23rd

Had breakfast at nine and had to be at the Castle by one. We had the Princess Helena and the Princess Louise for an hour, got home to dinner by half past two. Went back to the Castle at six and gave Prince Arthur a lesson, then the Princess Royal and the Princess Alice came and had their lesson. We got home by half past 7, had tea, and to bed by eleven.

X. WINDSOR, DECEMBER, 1856

Wednesday the 24th

Attendance at the Castle the same, and the same pupils as on the day previous. As there was to be no lesson on the 25th we went to London *for* Christmas Day.

Thursday the 25th

In London. After breakfast met Charly and Isabella by appointment. Drove to St Catherine's Dock and put Isabella on board an Antwerp steamer, then came back to Web's Hotel. Charlotte went to Kensington and I joined her at dinner in Mrs Robson's at five o'clock, got back to my hotel by ten and to bed by eleven.

Friday the 26th

Met Charlotte at ten next morning and drove *to* the Windsor Station *at* Waterloo. Got a train at quarter to eleven and arrived in Windsor at twelve. Then dressed and got to the Castle at one, gave the Princess Helena and the Princess Louise their lesson and got home to dinner before three. Got back to the Castle at six and gave Prince Arthur his lesson then the Princess Alice and Miss Byng had a lesson, got home before eight.

Saturday the 27th

Same hours and the same pupils at the Castle with the addition of Miss Cathcart. Got home before eight and met Mr F. Robson from London who came to spend a day with us.

Sunday the 28th

After breakfast Mr Robson, Charlotte and I had a long walk up to the Statue at the top of the Long Walk then round to the Datchet Gate up the side of the Thames to the Dairy Farm then to Mr McDonald's at the Fancy Dog Kennels. Had a glass of grog with McDonald, saw all the dogs and home to dinner at five o'clock. Mr McDonald called in the evening and we had some toddy. After he left we got to bed at eleven.

Monday the 29th

Had to be at the Castle by eight o'clock this morning for the younger Princesses, they having to sit to a portrait painter in the forenoon. Got home to breakfast before ten, walked about all day, had dinner, and as we went to the Castle at six, Mr F. Robson went off to London.

Tuesday the 30th

Attended in the forenoon for the younger Princesses and in the evening for the Princess Alice, Miss Byng and Miss Cathcart, and got home by seven.

No entry for Wednesday the 31st

Thursday the 1st

No lesson at the Castle this day, I went to dine with Mr Menzies at Park Side. Charlotte remained in Windsor expecting Lizzie. Mr Menzies had some friends and we spent a very happy evening, fiddling, singing and dancing. I got to Windsor next day by ten o'clock.

Friday the 2nd

Got to the Castle at one and gave the Princess Helena and the Princess Louise their lesson and home to dinner. Back again to the Castle at six and had all the Royal Children and ten or twelve strangers, children belonging to the Nobility in and about Windsor. They all had a dance together commencing with a Country Dance, Gayities and Gravities. And then Pop Goes the Weasel (to please the little ones). They all danced for an hour but none of them could dance a Reel, but the Royal Children. We then went and had tea with Mrs McDonald and got home by ten o'clock and to bed.

Saturday the 3rd

Gave a lesson to the younger Princesses at one, also a lesson with the skipping rope, and home to dinner before three. Back again to the Castle at five and gave Prince Arthur his lesson then the Princess Royal and the Princess Alice. The Princess Royal got a severe fall on the slippery floor and I had the honour of lifting her up. She was not hurt very much and continued her lesson. We got home by seven.

Sunday the 4th

Charlotte went to London by the eight am train expecting to meet Lizzie, and I walked up to Park Side to dine with Mr Menzies and drove back again at night in his pony phaeton and got to bed by ten o'clock.

Monday the 5th

Got to the castle at one, no lesson this forenoon. We went to the train expecting to meet Lizzie, were again disappointed. Came home to dinner, back to the Castle at six and gave Prince Arthur his lesson, then the

X. WINDSOR, DECEMBER, 1856–JANUARY, 1857

Princess Alice. The nurse brought Prince Leopold to see the dancing, he is a beautiful child. They then all had a romp with Charlotte and she led Prince Leopold through the Country Dance, Pop Goes the Weasel.

Tuesday the 6th Last lesson

Got to the Castle at one and gave the Princesses Helena and Louise their lesson, home to dinner at two and back to the Castle at five. After the Princess Alice had her lesson, Charlotte went off to London in great anxiety about Lizzie. At six o'clock Princess Helena, Princess Louise, Prince Arthur and Prince Leopold came in, Prince Arthur and the two Princesses took a short lesson, then the four had a regular romp for half an hour, and I got away before seven. This day Charlotte got some pretty presents from the children off the Queen's Christmas Tree.

Wednesday the 7th

Got up early and packed my luggage, went out and settled some bills, paid the lodgings, and started for London. Met Mr Menzies by chance at the station. We got a second class carriage to ourselves. I opened my fiddle box and fiddled all the way. Met Charlotte in Webb's Hotel, no word of Lizzie yet. Went to the wharf, telegraphed to Brussels, to see what had become of her. I then went to Gravesend to see Mr Davidson and Charlotte went to Kensington.

Thursday the 8th

On my arrival in London had a note saying that Lizzie had arrived safe. Went and dined at Mrs Robson's and saw her. From Mrs Robson's I went to spend the evening with Mr Lock and got to the hotel by two o'clock in the morning.

Friday the 9th

Met Charlotte, Lizzie, Miss Robson, her brother and Miss Laurier and we all went to spend the day at the Crystal Palace, then to the Haymarket Theatre at night.

Saturday the 10th

After breakfast we drove to King's Cross and got the train for Edinburgh and arrived safe about nine at night.

XI. Sixth Visit to Balmoral to Teach the Royal Children in 1857

Started from Inverness by the Nairn Railway at one am on the 20th September. From Nairn to Keith by the Coach and then by the Railway to Aberdeen. Arrived in Aberdeen at ten am. Drove to Douglas Hotel and had breakfast, then went to call for Mrs Alexander, after which I went and had a long walk to the Old Town to see the Colleges, down to the seaside, and lay about in The Links all forenoon, and back to Mrs Alexander's to dinner at four o'clock. Spent a very pleasant evening and got to the hotel by nine and went to bed.

Monday the 21st

Had breakfast by seven o'clock, and started by the Deeside Railway at a quarter before eight. Got to Banchory by half past nine and got the Coach up Deeside to Crathie and into my lodgings by four o'clock. Wrote a note to Miss Hildyard and Colonel Phipps announcing my arrival and went to bed by nine o'clock.

Tuesday the 22nd

Went to the Castle before nine to see Miss Hildyard, got word that there would be no lesson that day as the children were going out with the Queen, but, in a little, one of the Footmen came to me and told me that the Queen wished me to give a lesson to Prince Alfred at eleven. I went up to my lodgings for my fiddle and back again to the Castle, and met Prince Alfred and his Tutor in the New Ball Room, and gave him a long lesson. In going for my fiddle I met the Princess Royal on the road and she asked very kindly for me and my family. I dined at the Castle at two o'clock, took a long walk and got home to tea at seven, read and wrote this, then to bed by nine o'clock.

Wednesday the 23rd

Got to the Castle by appointment at eight am, gave the Princess Alice a lesson in Calisthenics, then to breakfast at nine. Before breakfast was over Lady Churchill, the Lady in Waiting, and the Hon. Miss Flora McDonald, Maid of Honour, sent for me to meet them in the Ball Room, and I gave them a long lesson in Scotch Steps. Price Alfred then came and had his lesson, then the younger Princesses Helena and Louise, with Prince Arthur, came and had their lesson. They all seemed exceedingly glad to see me again, and shook hands with me in the kindest manner. After their lesson I went to dinner at two o'clock. Before dinner was over Lady Churchill, Miss McDonald and Lord Granville sent for me to meet them in the Ball

XI. BALMORAL, SEPTEMBER, 1857

Room, and I gave the three a lesson for nearly an hour. Then went home and had tea. Went back again to the Castle at ten, to see the Servants' Ball, the Queen, the Prince, all the Royal Children with the Lords and Ladies in Waiting came into the Ball Room about half past ten, and all joined heartily in the dance, except the Queen and the Prince. The Queen could hardly keep her seat for laughing at Lord Granville's attempts to dance the Highland Fling, and the vigorous attempts of little Prince Arthur to dance the Steps he saw the Highlanders about him doing. The other children danced very nicely indeed, and were very much admired by all the people. The Queen and the Gentry remained about an hour and a half then left. I also left and came home to bed, but the Ball was kept up till three o'clock.

Thursday the 24th

Got to the Castle by eight, the Princess Alice was not ready and I gave no lesson this morning, and went in to breakfast. I then took a long walk and got back to meet Prince Alfred at eleven but he did not come, having gone to the hill to stalk deer for the first time. I waited in the Ball Room till one for the younger Princesses but they did not come. Prince Arthur came and had a short lesson. I went to dinner at two, before I finished dinner Lady Churchill and Miss McDonald sent for me. I met them in the Ball Room and gave them nearly an hour's lesson. I then went home and amused myself till ten and then to bed.

Friday the 25th

Got to the Castle by eight, and gave a lesson to the Princess Royal, Princess Alice and Prince Alfred. Then went in to breakfast and had nothing to do till one. I then had the Princess Louise and Prince Arthur and gave them a long lesson. When at the lesson, Prince Albert came into the room and danced away with little Prince Arthur, swung him about and was very funny and very pleasant. I then went to dinner, came back to the Ball Room and waited for an hour for Lady Churchill but she did not come and I went home. Met Ross the Piper and while walking along the road with him, the Queen, the Prince, Princess Alice and Prince Alfred came past. The Queen stopped and asked very kindly for me and my family, how the children were getting on &c &c. Then walked on and I came home, read the newspapers, wrote this Journal and to bed by ten o'clock.

Saturday the 26th

Got to the Castle at eight, gave the Princess Alice her usual lesson, then went to breakfast. Had nothing to do till one, I then had the Princess Helena and Prince Arthur for half an hour. Went to dinner at two, was sent for to

23. Prince Arthur, 1857

Arthur's birthday, 1 May 1850, was also the 81st birthday of the revered Duke of Wellington who became a godfather. The young Arthur was constantly reminded of his military destiny in watching the Changing of the Guard or a military band, and in presents of a toy drum, army uniform or map of a famous battle. His soldier training, begun in 1866, allowed him to mix well with people and maintain a military bearing which the Queen greatly admired when he accompanied her on state occasions. In 1857 Joseph Lowe notes the enjoyment the seven year old Prince Arthur has of a ball at Balmoral.

Photographer: Caldesi. Copyright Windsor Castle. Royal Archives. (c) 1991. Her Majesty The Queen.

XI. BALMORAL, SEPTEMBER, 1857.

meet Lady Churchill and Miss McDonald in the Ball Room. They had a lesson for nearly an hour then went away and I went home. On my way the Princess Royal and Miss Hildyard passed me in a carriage. The Princess called out "How do you do Mr Lowe," and in lifting my hat my gloves fell out and the Princess called out "You have dropped your gloves Mr Lowe" and pointed back over the carriage. I got home by four o'clock, and read, wrote, and fiddled the whole evening, and to bed by ten.

Sunday the 27th

Breakfasted at nine, then a long walk amongst the banks of Abergeldie. Got to the Castle to dinner by two then went and called for Mrs Chrystal, walked up the north side of the Dee to see the Castle from that direction. Went home and found Willie Blair waiting for me, went part of the way home with him, met Mr McDonald and Mr Gibbs and came back with them, and went to my lodgings and had tea and to bed by ten.

Monday the 28th

Got to the Castle by eight and gave the Princess Alice her lesson and then to breakfast. A message came by one of the Footmen that the Queen wanted to see me in the Drawing Room at twelve and *he* said don't be out of the way as I might be sent for sooner. I went *to* the Ball Room and waited. One of the Pages came to the Ball Room for me at twelve and said the Queen wish*es* you to bring your violin to the Drawing Room. When I went I met the Queen and Lady Churchill, Her Majesty was very affable and condescending and went over all her Reel Steps with great spirit in preparation for a Grand Ball that was to take place on the next evening. She complained very much of the music that they had and I offered to go into the orchestra to assist. Her Majesty thanked me and I told Lady Churchill that it would be necessary for one of the Pages to inform the Leader of the Band that the Queen wished me to be present to assist. I went to the Ball Room again, gave the Princess Helena, the Princess Louise and Prince Arthur their lesson, then went to dinner and got home by four o'clock. I took my fishing rod to the Distillery Pond to try if there were any trout in it and to my surprise I got a rise at the second cast. I now went to it in earnest and caught seven fine trout, got home to tea at seven and to bed by ten.

Tuesday the 29th

Got to the Castle at eight, and gave the Princess Alice her lesson, then went to breakfast. Went then to the Ball Room, and had Prince Alfred for half an hour, waited till one, then had the younger Princesses and Prince

Arthur, then to dinner. Got home by four, prepared some music for the Ball, went to the castle at seven, and waited till the Band arrived from Aberdeen. Mr Whiting, the Page, told the leader, Mr Granty, a German, that it was the Queen's wish that I should be in the Orchestra to assist, at which Mr Granty seemed not at all well pleased, and said that had he known that, he would not have come at all. But I made friends with him, and went into the Orchestra amongst fourteen strangers and took my seat beside the Leader and played off the same book with him. I saw at once that he knew very little about the business and I took the lead. We first played a Quadrille, The England, then there was a Reel to the pipes, then another Quadrille, then the Everlasting Jig, which none of them could play, except one man in a kind of way, but he could not continue and did not know the tunes so the whole rested on my one fiddle against all their vamping accompaniments. A very trying situation for me before the Queen and Court, but I rattled away at the Jigs and got through it better than might have been expected. There was then another Reel to the pipes then a long Country Dance which I had to do alone again, as none of them knew any Reels except this one man and he knew very few of them and his style was so very different from mine that he was often like to put me out so I began to play Reels that he did not know and got on better without him and kept it up for three quarters of an hour with the Leader of the Band lying over the back of my chair. He did not lift a fiddle all the time. My fiddle spoke out beautifully and I kept it up with spirit till the end. The Leader expressed himself surprised at my lasting qualities and at the power of my fiddle. The pipes then played another Reel, the Queen and all the company then stood up for Sir Roger de Coverley, which finished the Ball. This was played very badly indeed as none of them knew it, and the copy they had was quite different from my set of it. The band from Aberdeen only played two Quadrilles and nothing else the whole evening except trying to accompany me. Of course the music was not at all effective and could not have given satisfaction and I felt very sorry that I had anything to do with it. I went in with the others to a capital supper and plenty of wine. I left them at it and got home to bed by two in the morning.

Wednesday the 30th

No lesson at the Castle this morning. I breakfasted at home and got to the Castle at one and had the younger Princesses, then to dinner at two, and home before four. I went to the Distillery Pond to fish and caught eleven nice trout. I took a bag with me with a large flagon and kept them all alive as Prince Alfred asked me to do so when I got any, as he wished to put them in to the fountain in front of the Castle. When I sent them up to him he

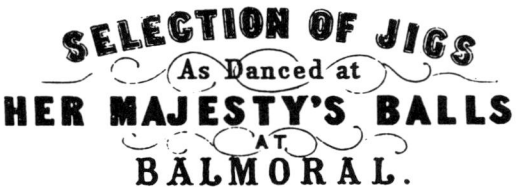

SIR ROGER DE COVERLY. Country Dance.

24. Sir Roger de Coverley

"Sir Roger de Coverly or the Haymakers.

"The Lady at the top, and Gentleman at the bottom, meet in the middle, turn by the right hand, and retire to places; the top Gentleman and bottom Lady do the same; the Lady at the top, and Gentleman at the bottom, meet in the middle, and, after turning by the left hand, retire to places; the top Gentleman and bottom Lady do the same; the first two then advance and turn with both hands, pass back to back and retire to places; the others do the same; the first two again advance, bow and curtsey, and retire to places; the others do the same; then the first couple turn off at the top, and all the others follow them, meeting partners at the bottom of the room, and leading up the centre; the first couple then make a half pousette with each couple till they reach the bottom of the dance, and they immediately begin with the second couple, which will then be at the top." (Instructions from *Lowes' Ball-Conductor* pages 103,104)

Queen Victoria's Journal 29th September 1857 gives some details of the Ball which Lowe, too preoccupied with the musical accompaniment, did not record:

"A nice dance in the Ball Room. Mrs Farquharson & large party came, 4 daughters & 6 sons, Ly. & Miss Bateman, Ld. Melville, Mr and Mrs Dundas, Mrs Gordon, Mr and Mrs G. and Miss Hope, Sir F., Ly. & Miss Thessiger, & and all our children there, busy dancing. We had Quadrilles, Reels, Country dances & a Perpetual Jig. Ld. Melville danced everything and was too amusing to look at."

took them to the Queen, *but* the Queen thought them too large for the fountain and ordered them to be killed and dressed for dinner.

Thursday the 1st

Got to the Castle at eight and gave all the usual lessons, had dinner at two and home by four. In going to fish again I met the Princess Alice and Miss Hildyard driving. They stopped and we had a long chat. The Princess asked me to catch some trout for her as she was so fond of them. I told her that if I got a few that I should send them to her but I only got four and did not think it worthwhile to send them, and had them fried for my own tea. I went to bed at ten.

Friday the 2nd

Got to the Castle at eight gave all the usual lessons and home by four. Nothing new this day.

Saturday the 3rd

A repetition of Friday

Sunday the 4th

Breakfasted at home and went to the Church at Crathie, Dr Robertson from Edinburgh preached. The Queen, the Prince, the Princess Royal, Lady Churchill and Miss Flora McDonald in the Queen's Seat. I went to the Castle to dinner, had a long walk and home to bed by nine o'clock.

Monday the 5th

Got to the Castle at the usual time and gave all the usual lessons and told them all that tomorrow would be the last lesson. Got home by four, wrote some tunes for Willie Blair and the Piper, went to bed at 10.

Tuesday the 6th Last Lesson

Got to the Castle at eight and gave the Princess Alice her last lesson. I then waited on Colonel Phipps to request a seat in the Messengers' Carriage to Perth. He told me "Most certainly Mr Lowe." I then went to the Ball Room and waited for the younger Princesses till one. They came and had their lesson, they shook hands and bade me goodbye and I went to dinner. I was sent for by Lady Churchill and Miss McDonald but after a short time the Queen sent for them and I went home to pack my portmanteaux. I had tea and went to bed by ten.

XI. BALMORAL, OCTOBER, 1857.

Wednesday the 7th Last Day

After breakfast I had my luggage taken to the Messengers' Carriage. In going beside Sandy McDonald with my luggage on his barrow, I met the Queen, Prince, Princess Royal, Princess Alice and Prince Alfred all walking together. They all stopped and spoke to me and wished me a safe journey. While packing my things in the Carriage they all came up and spoke with me again. The Queen asked me if I was going to Inverness or to Edinburgh and the Princesses desired to be kindly remembered to Charlotte and hoped that they would see her at Windsor at Christmas. Prince Albert told me in a joking way to see that no one got on top of my fiddle box which was strapped on the back of the carriage as they would be sure to crush them all to pieces. They then went away and I went up to the Castle to see some of my friends. The carriage started exactly at a quarter past eleven. I had a splendid ride through Braemar and got to Perth in time for the half past six train and was in my own house by a quarter past nine thus accomplishing the journey in ten hours.

XII. Visit to Windsor in 1857 and 1858 to Teach the Royal Children

Left Edinburgh by the quarter past nine train with Charlotte on Thursday the 24th of December. Got to London by eleven o'clock on the 25th, got a cab and drove to Webb's Hotel in Piccadilly where we had breakfast. Charlotte then dressed and went to see Mrs Robson at Kensington. Met George, he and I wandered about till 4 o'clock, then went to Webb's to get dinner. We then went to Astley's Theatre, from there to the Argyle Rooms to hear Pound Notes Band got home to the hotel by twelve o'clock and went to bed. Started on Saturday morning by eight o'clock to meet Mary from Brussels at St Catherine's Dock. After waiting for a long time the steamer came in. We then drove to the Waterloo Station, put Mary's boxes into the Luggage Room then went with her to Kensington to see Charlotte. We all stopped for dinner, George and I got back to Webb's by twelve o'clock and went to bed.

Sunday the 26th

Had breakfast at ten, wrote some letters for George then went out to walk. Returned to the hotel and had dinner, Charlotte and Mary came from Kensington, I drove them to the station and got the train for Windsor and arrived there by nine o'clock and found our lodgings quite ready for us, had some tea then went to bed.

Monday the 27th

Wrote a note to Miss Hildyard announcing our arrival, took it to the Castle and had an answer very soon after, desiring our attendance at four o'clock. Got to the Castle at four and had little Prince Leopold for his first lesson. We then had Prince Arthur then the Princesses Helena and Louise, remained with them till six o'clock then left and came home for Mary, and took her with us to tea at Mr McDonald's. We all got home by ten o'clock and went to bed.

Tuesday the 28th

Went to the Castle at one, and gave Prince Arthur a lesson in Exercises with the Clubs, got home to dinner at two returned to the castle with Charlotte at four. Had Prince Leopold first, then Prince Arthur, then the Princesses Helena and Louise. The Queen then came in and saw the Princesses take their lesson, Her Majesty then went over some of her Steps and was in great good humour, very affable and very gracious. She went up to Charlotte and asked very kindly for Jenny and the name of her husband

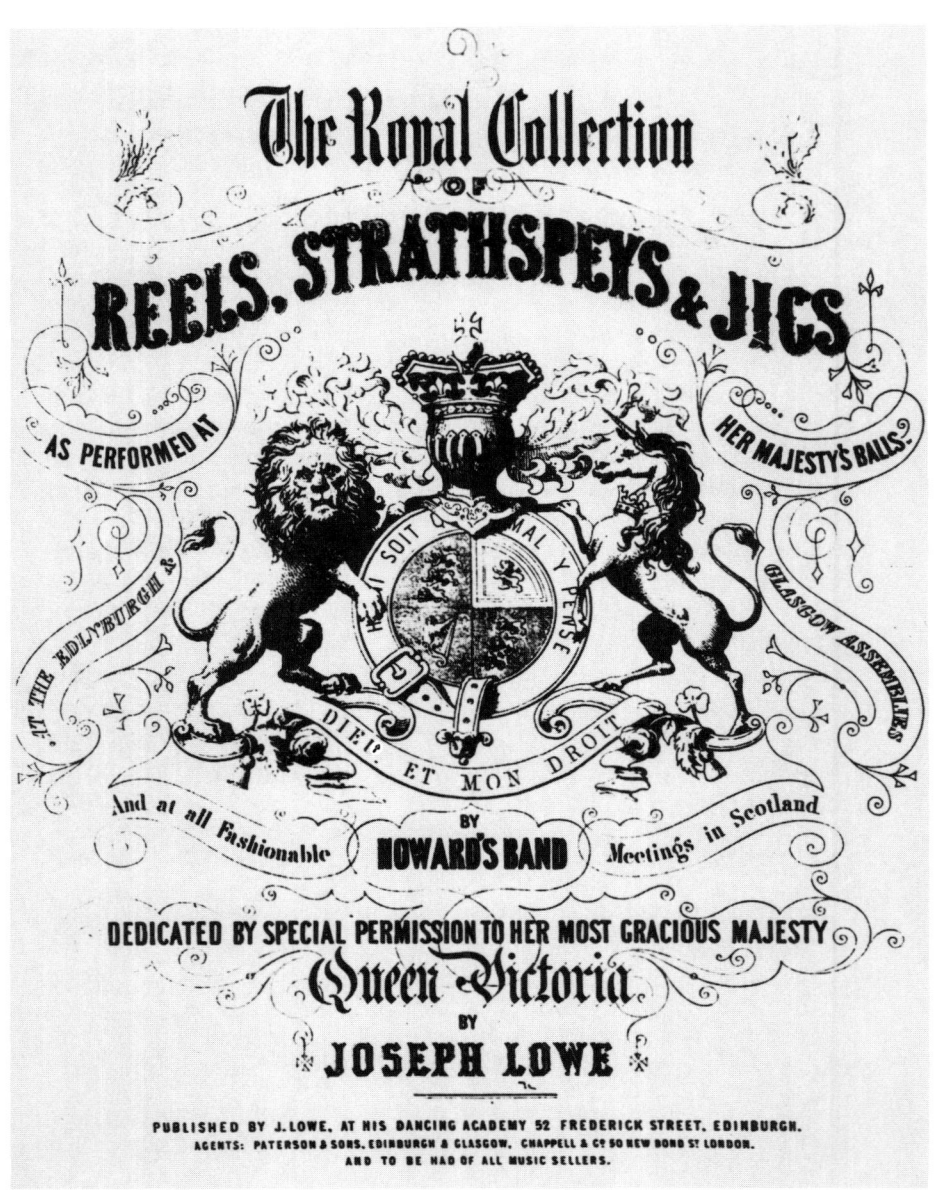

25. Title page of *The Royal Collection of Reels Strathspeys and Jigs*, 1859

The title page Joseph Lowe showed to the Queen on Friday 31st December 1857. This collection, of 300 items, is among the most extensive of the publications of Scottish music of the time. It is mentioned in the Obituary for Lowe that "the best class of our national music was arranged and published by him."

as she had forgotten it. When Charlotte told Her Majesty that Jenny had had a baby she seemed quite pleased and after a deal of talk she went away. The Princesses danced a little more then left, and we got home to tea and to bed.

Wednesday the 29th

Went to the Castle at four, had Prince Arthur and Prince Leopold then the Princesses Helena and Louise, then the Princess Alice came to see us, she being unwell could not dance. Nothing particular occurred and we got home by half past six.

Thursday the 30th

Got to the Castle by four o'clock. We were not long in the Drawing Room when the Queen came in expecting to meet the Princesses who had not yet come. Her Majesty went away immediately to look for them, and in a short time came back with the Princess Louise and Helena. Then Princess Alice, Prince Leopold and Prince Arthur came in. The Queen remained and saw the Princesses get their lesson, both in Dancing and Exercises. Her Majesty then asked Charlotte to show her a few of the exercises which she worked at for some time but complained of it tiring her arms, but she felt sure that it would do her much good as she was often annoyed with rheumatism in her arms. Her Majesty then danced a Reel with the Princess Alice, Princess Helena and my daughter. Then after a good deal of talk the Queen left and took the Princesses with her to dress. We were asked to wait as they would be back in half an hour. The Princesses Helena and Louise came and had a short lesson and we got home by half past six.

Friday the 31st

Got to the Castle at four, and had Prince Leopold then Prince Arthur, then the Princesses Alice, Helena, Louise and the Prince of Wales. The Prince came up directly to us and shook hands and asked how we had been since he last saw us. The younger Princesses had a good lesson and all of them left us wishing us a very Happy New Year. I had written a letter to Miss Hildyard wishing her to procure the Queen's patronage and to be allowed to dedicate my new book of Reels to Her Majesty and had a letter from Miss Hildyard the same evening stating that she had shown Her Majesty my sketch of the title page and Her Majesty accepted the dedication.

Saturday the 1st

No lesson at the Castle today. I got up at eight o'clock and went to be Mrs McDonald's First Foot and got home to breakfast before ten. Then took

XII. WINDSOR, JANUARY, 1858

Charlotte and Mary to the Riding School to see the Queen's presents given to the poor people in Windsor. From there we went to the Railway to meet George, after that I called on Colonel Biddulph to get tickets for the Grand Concert that was to take that night in St George's Hall. We all got in and were delighted with the music. All the greatest talent in London were in the orchestra which numbered about 200, including the choristers. Sims Reeves, and Miss Pine were the principal singers, the music was a selection from different operas. Before the concert began I found out the two Blagroves and took them to our lodging and had tea. The concert finished exactly at twelve.

Sunday the 2nd

Charlotte, Mary and George went out to walk, I being confined at home with inflammation in my left eye.

Monday the 3rd

Got to the Castle at four o'clock and gave the usual lessons. Then hired a cab and drove Charlotte and Mary up to Mr Menzies' in Windsor Forest to a Dancing Party and spent a very happy evening. Slept there all night.

Tuesday the 4th

After breakfast took a walk with Mary, a short way into the Forest to show her the scenery. On our return we got Mr Menzies' phaeton and drove back to Windsor. Had some dinner then dressed for the Castle, got there at four and gave the usual lessons, and got home by half past six, had tea and went early to bed.

Wednesday the 5th

Miss Robson and Eliza Lowe arrived from London as we were sitting down to dinner, of course a great deal of hugging and laughing. We got to the Castle at four and gave the usual lessons and got home to tea and spent a merry evening.

Thursday the 6th

Got to the Castle at four o'clock. The Queen came in with Princess Louise and saw her take her lesson. The Prince Consort then came in with the Princesses Alice and Helena. They all remained for some time then went away and Prince Arthur then came and had his lesson. The Princesses then came back and had a long lesson and we got home to tea at six o'clock. Charlotte then took Miss Robson, Mary and Eliza to show them over the

Castle. When they returned we had supper and some toddy, lots of laughing and fun then went to bed.

Friday the 7th

Miss Robson and Eliza went to London. We got to the Castle at the usual hour and gave the usual lessons.

Saturday the 8th, Last Lesson

Went out in the morning and paid all the accounts, made some calls and got to the Castle by four and gave the usual lessons. We were told that the Queen was to be present but she did not come. The Prince Consort came into the room looking for her but went away immediately when he saw that the Queen was not there. The Princess Alice brought in two portraits one of the Queen and one of the Prince and told me that they were sent to me by the Queen for my acceptance. Before they left they all kissed Charlotte and bade us both goodbye expressing a hope to meet us at Balmoral. We got home by half past six, packed our trunks and got early to bed.

Sunday the 9th

Got to London, Charlotte and Mary went to Kensington and I to my hotel.

Balmoral in 1858

Left Inverness with Mr Bushey, Balfour and Millar, on the 19th Septr 1858 to play a Ball at Balmoral on the 20th, got to Aberdeen on the 20th to Breakfast, it being Sunday had to stop all day in Aberdeen, then took the train up Dee side to Banchory on the Monday Morning and then the coach from Banchory to Balmoral, got there by 3 oclock put our Instruments into the Orchestra then went to secure Beds in the village got Supper and back to the Castle by 9 Oclock, went into the Orchestra and tuned and waited till 10 when the Royal party came into the Ball Room as they entered we played God Save the Queen, we were then asked to play a Quadrille, then followed a Reel to the Bagpipes, then another Quadrille then a Reel, then a Country Dance, a Reel to the Bagpipes, an Irish Jig then Sir Roger de Coverly which finished the Ball, we then went to the Stewards Room and had a good supper

26. The Journal of Joseph Lowe, facsimile page: "Balmoral in 1858"
Queen Victoria describes the Ball in her Journal 20th September 1858.

"We had a pretty Ball in the Ball Room, the decoration of which is now finished & really beautiful. The 3 younger children appeared. Besides Ross, playing the Pipes, Mr Lowe brought a small Band. We had 2 Quadrilles, 4 Reels, a Perpetual Jig, & 2 Country dances. Very gay. All over by 1. Poor Sir C. Phipps had such a fall in Sir R. de Coverley."

XIII. Balmoral in 1858

Left Inverness with Mr Bushey, Balfour and Millar on the 19th September 1858 to play a Ball at Balmoral on the 20th. Got to Aberdeen *for* breakfast. It being Sunday, had to stop all day in Aberdeen, then took the train up Deeside to Banchory on the Monday morning and then the coach from Banchory to Balmoral. Got there by 3 o'clock, put our instruments into the orchestra then went to secure beds in the village. Got dressed and back to the Castle by nine o'clock. Went into the orchestra and tuned and waited till ten when the Royal Party came into the Ball Room. As they entered we played God Save the Queen. We were then asked to play a Quadrille, then followed a Reel to the bagpipes, then another Quadrille, then a Reel, then a Country Dance, a Reel to the bagpipes, an Irish Jig, then Sir Roger de Coverley which finished the Ball, we then went to the Stewards' Room and had a good supper and plenty of wine and then off to the village to bed.

Tuesday the 21st

Got up in the morning and saw the men off by the coach, then went to my lodgings and had breakfast, wrote a note to Miss Hildyard, saw her in the afternoon and got Orders to be at the Castle to commence my lessons at half past eight o'clock next morning. Had a good dinner then walked about all the evening and to bed by eight o'clock.

Wednesday the 22nd

Got to the Castle by half past eight, gave the Princess Helena an Exercise lesson then had breakfast at the Castle. Got Orders to be in the Ball Room by half past twelve, I then had the Princesses Alice and Helena, for a Dancing lesson, then had the Princess Louise and Prince Arthur for their lesson, then went to dinner, nothing more to do this day.

Thursday the 23rd

The same as the day before.

Friday the 24th

The same.

Saturday the 25th

The same.

Sunday the 26th

Took some medicine and did not go to Church. The 26th, 27th, 28th, 29th and 30th the usual lessons every day. Nothing particular occurred except that the Queen passed me in her carriage and said "How do you do, Mr Lowe," the Prince took off his cap. Nothing particular occurred this season till the end.

27. Interior of a tent erected at Balmoral for a Ball, 1868

A tent erected at Balmoral for a Ball in 1868. On the dais, from left, the Duchess of Atholl, Princess Beatrice, Queen Victoria, Princess Louise, the Prince of Wales, Prince Leopold, and Prince Arthur.

In Scotland in the 18th century it was customary for the Laird to hold a Ball for tenants on the Estate and neighbours. Queen Victoria continued this tradition at Balmoral and describes a Ball in her Journal for 29th September 1858.

"At 10 we went down to the Ball Room, where there was a very gay Gillies Ball. Our children all danced a great deal, including Arthur, who showed that he had profited by Mr Lowe's lessons, making such exertions in his steps, & in a jig taking courage & cutting out several. He was universally applauded. We stayed till 1, but the dancing went on till near 4 !"

Photographer: W & D Downey. Copyright Windsor Castle. Royal Archives. (c) 1991. Her Majesty The Queen.

XIV. Visit to Windsor Castle in 1859 and 1860 to Teach the Royal Children

Left Edinburgh with my daughter Charlotte on Tuesday 20th of December 1859 by the half to nine train, had to go round by Kelso on account of the rails being shut up by the snow. Got to Berwick three hours behind the usual time and did not get to York till six am, did not get to London till twelve. Drove directly to the Waterloo Station and got a train to Windsor where we arrived on the Wednesday at three pm. Found our lodgings ready, then wrote a note to Miss Hildyard announcing our arrival. Went out and made some purchases in the shape of tea, sugar, and candles &c &c, hired a piano then came home and tea and to bed by nine o'clock.

Thursday the 22nd

Breakfasted at ten, we had a note from Miss Hildyard to say that Prince Leopold would be ready for a lesson in the Red Drawing Room at one, and the Princesses Helena and Louise at half past one. Got to the Castle in time and gave the lessons and got Orders to be back again for the Princess Louise, Princes Arthur and Leopold at half past five. Gave them a good long lesson and got to our lodging by seven and had tea.

Friday the 23rd

The same attendance and the same lessons as on the previous day.

Saturday the 24th

Gave the same lessons in the forenoon, no lesson in the evening. Charlotte went to London and I came home to dinner. Had Ross the Piper with me in the evening, and had music and toddy, but got to bed by twelve o'clock.

Sunday the 25th

Went to dine with Mr Ross at one o'clock, then came home and remained in the house all afternoon owing to the very wet day.

Monday the 26th

Went to meet Charlotte at the Station. Came home and dressed and got to the Castle by one. Gave the Princess Helena and the Prince Leopold a lesson, and got home to dinner by two. Went back to the Castle at half past five, had the Princes Arthur and Leopold, then the Princesses Helena and Louise. The Queen then came in with the Princess Alice, they all danced together for some time then went away. We got home by half past seven

XIV. WINDSOR, DECEMBER, 1859–JANUARY, 1860

and dressed for a party at Mr Menzies' at Park Side, four miles from Windsor. Hired a cab to take us there and bring us back. We spent a very pleasant evening and got back to Windsor by four in the morning.

Tuesday the 27th

Same lessons at the Castle as on the previous day. Eliza Lowe came from London to pay us a visit.

Wednesday the 28th

Same lessons in the forenoon as on the Tuesday. In the evening we had the whole of the Royal Family including the Queen, Prince of Wales &c &c. They all danced together for an hour, my daughter with them, and often a dispute who should have her for a partner. The whole of them left and we got home by half past seven and had tea, played at cards and then to bed.
The 29th, 30th and 31st same lessons as on the previous days, nothing particular.

Monday the 2nd

Took Eliza to the Riding School in the morning to see the charities given to the poor people in Windsor. Got to the Castle at one, and gave the usual lessons. Back again at five to meet Miss Byng and Miss Cathcart. Gave them a lesson, then had the Princesses till seven and got home by half past seven to tea.

Tuesday the 3rd

Gave the usual lessons in the morning and home to dinner by two. Back to the Castle again at five for Miss Byng, then had Prince Arthur and Prince Leopold then the Princesses. The Queen then came in with Princess Alice and the Prince of Wales, they all danced together for an hour. The Queen, the Princess Alice, Prince of Wales and my daughter danced the Reel of Tulloch with great spirit, swinging each other without ceremony sometimes rather too roughly and with too much force for such a slippery floor, but they all seemed to enjoy it very much. They then went away and we got home by seven.

Wednesday the 4th

Went to the Castle in the morning by invitation to see a Review where the Queen gave the Victoria Cross to a number of Officers and men who had distinguished themselves in India, a grand and very interesting sight.

Several poor fellows not recovered from their wounds (in plain clothes) could hardly walk up to the Queen to receive their medals. When the medals were all given out the soldiers all marched past the Queen and out of the Quadrangle. After the Review we went to the Drawing Room and had Prince Leopold for his lesson and got home to dinner at two. Went back to the Castle at five, and give the Princesses their lesson. The Queen also came and had a dance with the others for half an hour, then went away and we got home by seven. Mr Weddell, the Master of the Life Guards Band, called and we spent a pleasant evening and got to bed by eleven o'clock.

Thursday the 5th, Last Lesson

Got to the Castle at half past twelve to meet Miss Byng. We then had the Princess Louise and Prince Leopold for their lesson. We got home to dinner by two, went back in the evening and had all the Royal Family. They danced for nearly two hours then bade us goodbye, we went home and packed our trunks. In the morning I went and settled all accounts, got to the Station by two and off to London. Charlotte went to Kensington, I to the hotel. Stayed in London till Monday evening, then took the night train home to Edinburgh.

XV. Balmoral in 1860

Started by myself from Inverness on the 20th of August. Was to meet Charlotte in Aberdeen by appointment on that day, she did not come and I took the train to Aboyne, expecting to meet her there. She came by the next train and we remained there all night, and went by the Coach to Balmoral next day. Mrs Chrystal could not take us in as she had promised but got us a lodging at McKenzie's farm on the face of the hill. Prince Leopold had sprained his ankle, and the others were so much engaged that we only gave ten lessons in all this season. Nothing particular occurred during our stay worth mentioning and we got away, Charlotte coming to Edinburgh and I returning to Inverness for the Northern Meeting.

28. Royal Family Group, Buckingham Palace, February 29th 1860.
From left, Prince Leopold, Princess Louise, Prince Alfred, Princess Alice and Princess Helena.
Photographer: Colonel Hon. Dudley de Ros. Copyright Windsor Castle. Royal Archives. (c) 1991. Her Majesty The Queen.

XVI. Visit to Windsor Castle in 1860 and 1861

Left Edinburgh by the four o'clock train for Liverpool on the 19th of December during a very heavy snow storm. We stuck fast several times before we got to Carstairs Junction and was seven hours before we got to that station. We then got on pretty well but did not reach Liverpool till eight in the morning, eight hours behind the usual time. We went to a hotel and had breakfast, then took a cab and drove to my nephew's, John Lowe. After sitting for some time we had a cab and drove to the Albert Docks to see my son John, who had just arrived from British Columbia on board his ship. After parting with him we went to call upon Mr Stewart. After spending some time with him we went to Birkenhead to call for Mr Wolverton but did not find him at home, left a note of our address. We then came home to dine with John my nephew. Mr & Mrs Stewart came in the evening and also Mr Wolverton. We spent a very pleasant evening and when they left we all went to bed. I slept at Mr Stewart's and Charlotte at John's. Next day I went to the Docks to meet Captain Bracey by appointment, had a deal of talk with him about John, he not liking Captain Bracey's ship. I got up his indenture and made him free to join another ship. We all dined with Mr Stewart and in the evening went to a concert in St James' Hall, from that we went home to bed. On the Saturday morning met Charlotte at the Railway and drove to the Ferry, crossed and took the Railway from Birkenhead through part of Wales by Leamington, Birmingham, Brandbury, Oxford and Reading and got a train from there to Windsor where we arrived at ten o'clock four hours behind time. Found our lodgings quite ready, had tea then went to bed. Sunday morning we announced our arrival at the Castle, and had an answer from Miss Hildyard that the Princesses could not take a lesson till Wednesday. We sent to Slough and called for Mrs McDonald and got home by ten o'clock and to bed. Tuesday went and brought in provisions, hired piano &c &c.

Wednesday the 26th

Got to the Castle at five and had the little Princess Beatrice but found her too young and could not learn anything Prince Leopold then had a lesson, then Prince Arthur, then the Princesses Helena, Louise and the Prince of Wales came. They all danced a Reel, then the Reel of Tulloch with Charlotte, she and the Prince of Wales were the Gentlemen, they had a nice swing, they then all together danced The Lancers. The Princesses did their Exercises, and the different sets of Steps, then all went away. We got home by seven o'clock.

XVI. WINDSOR, DECEMBER, 1860

Thursday the 27th

Attended at the usual hour, gave all the usual lessons. Got home at the usual hour and nothing unusual occurred.

Friday the 28th

Got to the Castle at the same hour, and all the lessons the same as on the preceding days, Miss Laurier came to spend a few days with Charlotte, Mrs James Lowe also arrived to pay us a visit.

Saturday the 29th

Got to the Castle at the same time, and gave the usual lessons. The Queen and the Princess Alice came to see us this evening and remained for a long time. They had a good laugh at the Princess Beatrice attempting to do her Positions, when they all left we got home to tea.

Sunday the 30th

Went to Church in the forenoon, then hired a cab and took Miss Laurier and Charlotte to Slough to dine with Mrs McDonald (a dreadfully bad day). We spent a very agreeable evening, the cab came for us and we got home by ten o'clock.

Monday the 31st

The same lessons as on the other days. No more lessons this season, as all the family had arranged to go to Osborne on the Wednesday so we started for London on the Tuesday evening and put up in a hotel in Air Street, Miss Laurier sleeping with Charlotte. Remained in London for a few days, and visited Mr Locke and Mr Grant and got back to Edinburgh on Sunday morning by eight o'clock.

APPENDICES

APPENDIX 1. OBITUARY

The Late Mr Joseph Lowe

The Inverness Courier says : -

"Many of our readers in all parts of the world will be concerned to hear of the death of Mr. Lowe, Edinburgh, which happened suddenly at North Berwick on Thursday last. Mr.Lowe had been suffering for several years from the effects of more than one paralytic attack, and also from enlargement of the heart, the latter probably being the immediate cause of his sudden death. For nearly forty years Mr.Lowe visited Inverness every summer as a teacher of dancing; he was universally recognised as the head of his profession, and statedly visited Balmoral as teacher of the Royal family - an office to which the Misses Lowe succeeded when their father retired from business. The deceased was an accomplished musician; some of the most popular reels and strathspeys of modern days are his compositions, and the best collection of this class of our national music was arranged and published by him. Mr.Lowe was also author of several excellent songs, chiefly piscatorial, one or two of which have been published in the annual of the Edinburgh Angling Club. As a fisher his name is known from Tweed to Thurso, and those who have ever enjoyed a day on the river side with this keen angler and genial companion will never forget his merry laugh, his quaint stories, and his indominatable buoyancy of spirit. Mr.Lowe will be long remembered and regretted by a very wide circle of friends." Mr.Lowe was a native of Brechin.

The Brechin Advertiser, 24 July 1866.

APPENDIX 2. "THE BALMORAL CASTLE QUADRILLE" BY JOSEPH LOWE

PUSH ABOUT THE JORUM.

FAVOURITE GAELIC AIR.
GU MA SLÀN A CHÌ MI, MO CHAILINN DÌLEAS DONN.

CODA.

Lowe's Balmoral Castle Quadrille.

APPENDIX 2. "THE BALMORAL CASTLE QUADRILLE"

THERE CAME A YOUNG MAN TO MY DADDIE'S DOOR.

COCK UP YOUR BEAVER.

Lowe's Balmoral Castle Quadrille.

OH THIS IS NO MY AIN LASSIE FAIR THO' THE LASSIE BE.

Nº 4.

Lowe's Balmoral Castle Quadrille.

APPENDIX 2. "THE BALMORAL CASTLE QUADRILLE"

Lowes Balmoral Castle Quadrille.

APPENDIX 2. "THE BALMORAL CASTLE QUADRILLE"

THE JOURNAL OF JOSEPH LOWE

8

THE QUEEN'S WELCOME TO DEE SIDE.   STRATHSPEY.   by Jos. Lowe.

PRINCE ALBERT'S REEL.   by Jos. Lowe.

Lowe's Balmoral Castle Quadrille.

APPENDIX 3a. THE ROYAL FAMILY ASSOCIATED WITH THE JOURNAL OF JOSEPH LOWE

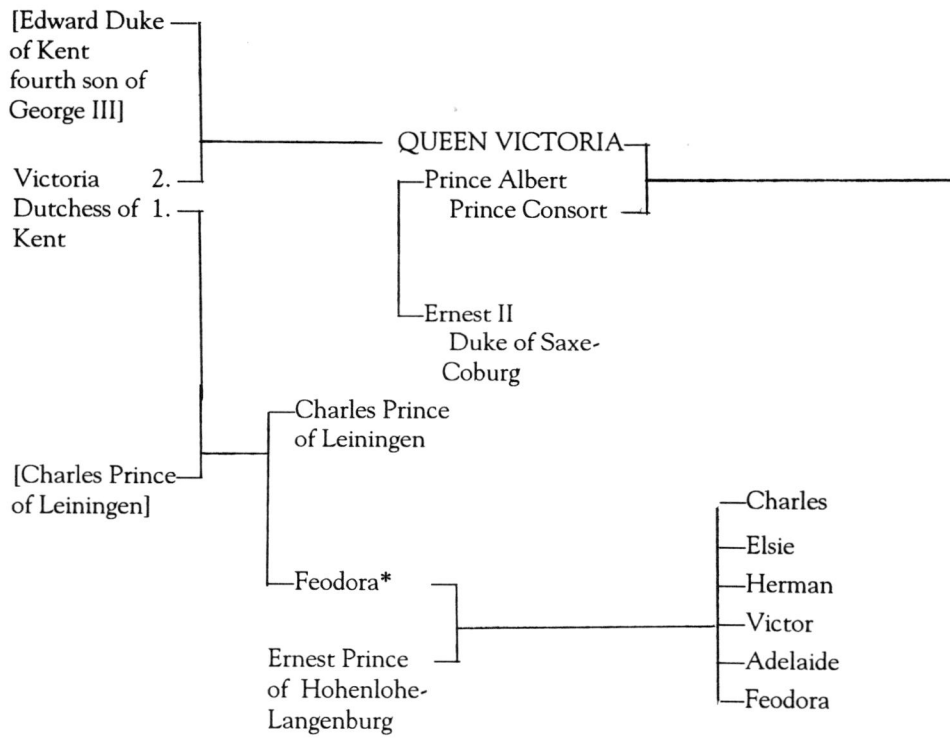

*The family of Queen Victoria's half-sister were at Abergeldie during the first visit of Mr. Lowe to Balmoral.

The German relations, Charles, Ernest and Ernest II, are present later in the Journal as visitors to Balmoral.

- Princess Royal b. 21 November 1840
  Victoria
  m. Prince Frederick William
  Frederick III German Emperor
- Prince of Wales b. 9 November 1841
  Albert Edward, EDWARD VIII
  m. Princess Alexandra of Denmark
- Princess Alice b. 25 April 1843
  m. Grand Duke of Hesse and by Rhine
- Prince Alfred b. 6 August 1844
  Duke of Edinburgh
  m. Grand Dutchess Marie of Russia
- Princess Helena b. 25 May 1846
  m. Prince Christian of Schleswig-Holstein
- Princess Louise b. 18 March 1848
  m. John Marquess of Lorne, later Duke of Argyll
- Prince Arthur b. 1 May 1850
  Duke of Connaught
  m. Princess Louise Margaret of Russia
- Prince Leopold b. 7 April 1853
  Duke of Albany
  m. Princess Helen of Waldeck-Pyrmont
- Princess Beatrice b. 14 April 1857
  m. Prince Henry of Battenburg

APPENDIX 3b. THREE GENERATIONS OF THE LOWE FAMILY

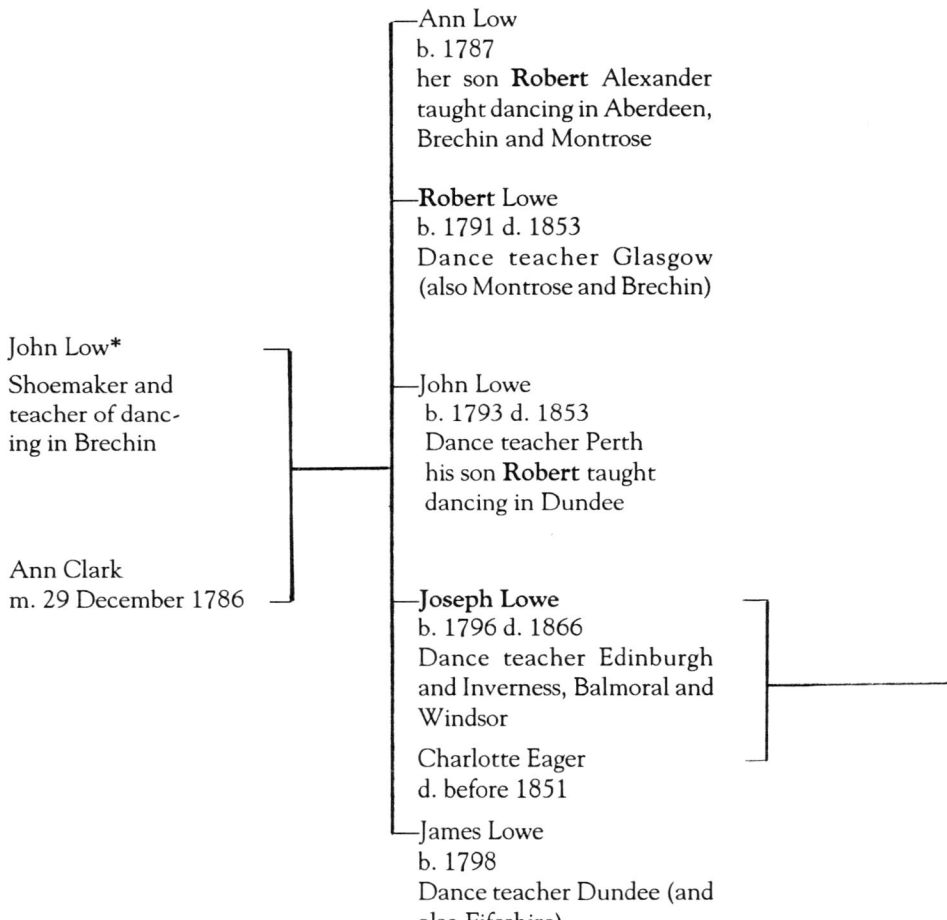

John Low*
Shoemaker and teacher of dancing in Brechin

Ann Clark
m. 29 December 1786

— Ann Low
b. 1787
her son **Robert** Alexander taught dancing in Aberdeen, Brechin and Montrose

— **Robert** Lowe
b. 1791 d. 1853
Dance teacher Glasgow (also Montrose and Brechin)

— John Lowe
b. 1793 d. 1853
Dance teacher Perth
his son **Robert** taught dancing in Dundee

— **Joseph Lowe**
b. 1796 d. 1866
Dance teacher Edinburgh and Inverness, Balmoral and Windsor

Charlotte Eager
d. before 1851

— James Lowe
b. 1798
Dance teacher Dundee (and also Fifeshire)

*Descendents of John Low added 'e' to the surname.

Compiled from marriage registers and information from Dr. Alastair MacFadyen. Those mentioned in the Journal of Joseph Lowe are in bold type.

THE JOURNAL OF JOSEPH LOWE

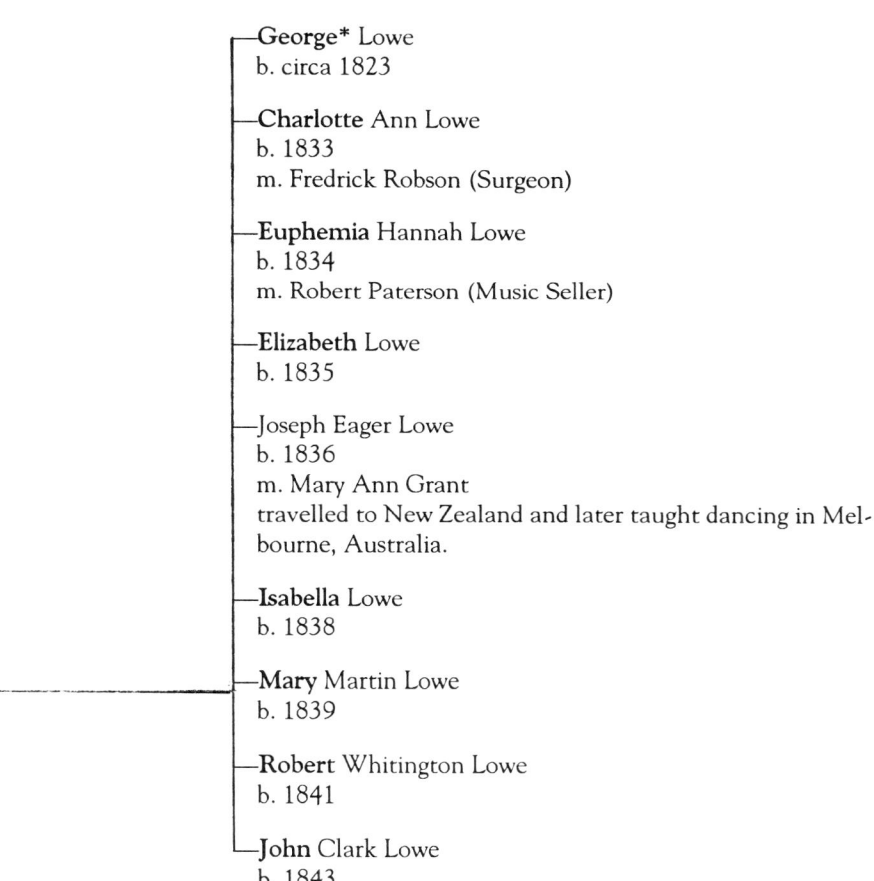

- **George*** Lowe
  b. circa 1823

- **Charlotte** Ann Lowe
  b. 1833
  m. Fredrick Robson (Surgeon)

- **Euphemia** Hannah Lowe
  b. 1834
  m. Robert Paterson (Music Seller)

- **Elizabeth** Lowe
  b. 1835

- Joseph Eager Lowe
  b. 1836
  m. Mary Ann Grant
  travelled to New Zealand and later taught dancing in Melbourne, Australia.

- **Isabella** Lowe
  b. 1838

- **Mary** Martin Lowe
  b. 1839

- **Robert** Whitington Lowe
  b. 1841

- **John** Clark Lowe
  b. 1843

*George is a son of Joseph Lowe, probably from an earlier marriage.

More details on the Lowe family of dance teachers in Scotland and New Zealand will be given in a publication associated with an Exhibition of the Lowe Collection of dance manuscripts and books at the National Library of New Zealand late in 1992.

APPENDIX 4. MEMBERS OF THE ROYAL HOUSEHOLD MENTIONED IN THE LOWE JOURNAL

Barrington	Lady Caroline Barrington; (Woman of the Bedchamber 1837-1875 also Superintendent of the Royal Princesses from 1851).
Baylis	Edward Baylis (employed in Royal Kitchens (1828-1854).
Becker	Dr Ernst Becker (Librarian to the Prince Consort 1851-1858).
Biddulph	Col. Biddulph (Master of the Household 1851-1866; Later Keeper of the Privy Purse).
Bruce	Lady Augusta Bruce (Lady in Waiting to the Duchess of Kent 1846-1861). Later a Woman of the Bedchamber to the Queen.
Bulteel	Miss Bulteel, Hon. Mary Bulteel (Maid of Honour 1853-1861).
Byng	Hon. Beatrice Byng (Maid of Honour 1851-1863)
Canning	Lady Canning (Lady of the Bedchamber 1842-1855).
Cathcart	Hon. Emily Cathcart (Maid of Honour 1855-1880). Later a Woman of the Bedchamber to the Queen.
Churchill	Jane, Lady Churchill (Lady of the Bedchamber 1854-1900).
Clark	Sir James Clark (Physician in Ordinary to the Queen 1837-1876).
Couper	Sir George Couper (Comptroller to the Duchess of Kent 1840-1861).
Ely	Lady Ely, Marchioness of Ely (Lady of the Bedchamber 1851-1889).
Gibbs	Frederick Gibbs (Tutor to the Prince of Wales 1851-1858).
Gibbs	Henry Gibbs (Sergeant Footman 1854-1861). Later a Messenger and a State Porter.
Hildyard	Miss Sarah Hildyard (Governess 1847-1865).
Illhardt	Miss Agnes Illhardt (German Governess 1850-1858).
Jocelyn	Lady Jocelyn, Viscountess Jocelyn (Lady of the Bedchamber 1841-1867).

Kerr	Hon. Lucy Kerr (Maid of Honour 1844-1872)
Mackay	Angus Mackay (Queen's Piper 1843-1853).
McDonald	Hon. Flora McDonald (Maid of Honour 1847-1874).
McDonald	John McDonald (Prince Albert's Highland Jäger 1847-1860).
Miller	Charles Miller (Clerk Comptroller of the Kitchen 1828-1866).
Phipps	Col. (from 1858 Sir) Charles Phipps (Keeper of the Privy Purse 1849 - 1866).
Renwick	Robert Renwick (Sergeant Footman 1844-1859; Gentleman Porter 1855-1862).
Roberts	John Roberts (Inspector of Windsor Castle 1845-1861).
Rollande	Mme. Louise Rollande (French Governess to the Royal Children 1847–1859).
Ross	William Ross (Queen's Piper 1854-1891).
Seabrook	William Seabrook (Steward to the Duchess of Kent c.1834-1861). Later Inspector at Windsor Castle.
Seymour	Col. Seymour (Equerry to Prince Albert 1846-1858). Later other Household positions.
Seymour	Hon. Florence Seymour (Maid of Honour 1864–1870).
Stockman	Dr Christian (Baron) Stockman. No official position in England; Private Secretary to Queen Victoria's uncle, King Leopold of Belgium, arranged the first meeting of Albert and Victoria, and remained an important advisor especially on the Children's education.

APPENDIX 5. MUSIC AND DANCE INDEX

Balls, 34, 46, 53, 75, 76, 94, 97, 98, 106, 107, 110
Balmoral Castle Quadrille, 75, 80, 81, Appendix 2 (pp. 118-25)
Bonny Braes O Mar, 45-46
Concerts, 35, 36, 66, 67, 104
Country Dance, 8, 35, 53, 55, 56, 91, 97, 107
Draw the Sword Scotland, 51
England, The (a Quadrille), 97
Everlasting Jig, The, 97
Exercises (only lessons with specific type of exercise), 24, 25, 33, 37, 43, 45, 55, 59, 91, 101
Fiddling, 33, 41, 44, 55, 59, 60, 61, 63, 64, 68, 70, 77, 81, 83, 87, 91, 92, 96, 104, 109
God Save the Queen, 39, 41, 67, 107
Gayities and Gravities, 51, 92
Highland Fling, 47, 61, 95
Irish Steps, 30, 40, 67
Jig, 75, 97, 107
La Grace, 83
Lady of the Lake (Country Dance), 27, 33, 38, 44, 51
Lancers, The, 113
Lass of Gowrie [Gourie], The, 87
Lowes' Ball-Conductor and Assembly Guide, 5, 6, 23, 98
Lowes' Royal Collection . . . , 28, 102, 103
Musicians, 2, 3
   Mackay, 29, 36, 38, 76
   Ross, 82
   Blair, 43, 46, 82 (*see also* Fiddling)
Music Instruments, 3, 35, 50, 63, 87, 89, 100, 109, 113
Music lessons (for Prince Alfred and John Lowe), 40, 41, 43, 44, 46, 60, 61, 93

Music writing, 3
   for Prince Alfred, 61
   for Willie Blair, 99
   Dedications, 102, 103 *see also* The Balmoral Castle Quadrille, pp. 118-25

Petronella, 44

Pig's March, 39, 87

Polka, 44

Pop Goes the Weasel, 11, 55, 65, 87, 91, 92

Princess Royal's Country Dance, 36

Prince of Wales Jig, 48

Prince Alfred's Reel, 42

Princess Alice's Jig, 38

Prince Arthur's First Jig in 1858, 95

Quadrille, 24, 30, 33, 38, 65, 97, 107

Reel of Eight, 27

Reel of Thulican, 28, 30, 43, 44

Reel of Tulloch, 27, 28, 34, 35, 51, 53, 55, 80, 83, 110, 113

Reels, 1, 8, 26, 33, 35, 43, 44, 46, 51, 53, 55, 56, 60, 65, 67, 74, 75, 80, 84, 87, 91, 97, 103, 107, 113

Reel Steps and Figures, 9, 22, 24, 25, 27, 34, 51, 93, 96

Reel of Three, 83, 86

Sir Roger de Coverley, 97, 98, 107

Spanish Guaracha, 11, 84, 86, 87

Sword Dance, 75

Victoria (Dance Lessons), 25, 27, 47, 51, 67, 80, 81, 85, 86, 101, 103

Waltz, 8, 44, 53, 55, 67, 68

BIBLIOGRAPHY

Bennett, Daphne, *Queen Victoria's Children*. London: Gollancz, 1980.

Diamond, Frances, & Roger Taylor, *Crown & Camera, The Royal Family and Photography 1842-1910*. London: Longmans, 1987.

Emmerson, George S. *Rantin' Pipe and Tremblin' String : A History of Scottish Dance Music* London: J.M.Dent and Son, 1971

____ . *A Social History of Scottish Dance. Ane Celestial Recreatioun*, Montreal and London McGill-Queen's University Press, 1972.

Fairbairn, Neil, and Clive Unger-Hamilton, *Royal Collection, An historic album of music composed exclusively by Members of the Royal Family*, London: Novello, 1977.

Flett, J.E. & T.M., *The History of the Scottish Reel as a Dance-Form*, Scottish Studies Volume 16, part 2, pages 91 - 119. 1972

____ . *Traditional Dancing in Scotland*, London: Routledge & Kegan Paul, 1985 (First Published 1964).

Gernsheim, Helmut and Alison, *Queen Victoria, A Biography in Word and Picture*, London: Longmans, 1959.

Hardie, Alastair J., *The Caledonian Companion*, London: EMI Music, 1981.

Johnson, David, *Scottish Fiddle Music in the 18th century*, London: John Donald, 1984.

Lowe, Joseph, *Royal Collection of Reels, Strathspeys & Jigs*. Edinburgh: Lowe\Patterson & Sons, [1895]

Lowe, Messrs. [J., R., J., and J.S., *Lowes' Ball-Conductor and Assembly Guide*, (Third Edition), Edinburgh: Lowe, [c. 1830].

Thomson, Andrew, "Note of a residence at Balmoral Castle, August 1849," Manuscript, Windsor: Royal Archives, 1849.

Victoria, Queen, "Our Life in the Highlands" [compilation of Leaves from the *Journal of Our Life in the Highlands*, 1868 and More Leaves...1884] London: William Kimber, 1968.

Woodham-Smith, Cecil, *Queen Victoria Her Life and Times, Volume One 1819-1861* London: Hamish Hamilton, 1972.

Information from Marriage Certificates, Ball Programmes, Miscellaneous Music, Newspapers and other Ephemera not individually listed.